BEST START

'This brilliant little book brings together the author's years of experience as a clinical psychologist helping parents manage the complexities of parenting, her anecdotes and stories from her living laboratory as a mother, informed by contemporary understanding from research in brain development and social science fields. I couldn't put this book down. Lynn's passion and expertise with parenting and child development shines through. Her book is like a lighthouse, providing clear guidance and clarity for anyone wanting to provide the best environment for a child to reach their full potential.'

Carolyn Hastie, midwife, educator and author
of thinkbirth.blogspot.com

'*Best Start* is a very practical book for parents. It doesn't spend time telling you how to parent, instead it gets people thinking about how to help their children grow-up feeling good about themselves. Lynn has used her own experiences as a parent mixed with her clinical skills to present a book that is witty and humorous as well as managing to cover very important areas such as emotional regulation and teaching the language of emotion to children.'

Julie Ferguson, nurse practitioner in the
field of perinatal mental health

'This is a comprehensive guide to an infant's emotional and social developmental needs ... ideal for parents interested in the deeper psychological needs of their babies.'

— Dr Beth Mah B.Med (Hons), F.R.A.N.Z.C.P., Cert.
Child Adol. Psych., Infant and Parent Psychiatrist

Understanding your baby's emotional needs to create the best beginnings

Lynn Jenkins
BA (Hons), MPsych (Clin)

PUBLISHING

First published 2012

Exisle Publishing Pty Ltd
'Moonrising', Narone Creek Road, Wollombi, NSW 2325, Australia
P.O. Box 60–490, Titirangi, Auckland 0642, New Zealand
www.exislepublishing.com

National Library of Australia Cataloguing-in-Publication Data:

Jenkins, Lynette Fay.

Best start : understanding your baby's emotional needs to create the best beginnings / Lynn Jenkins.

ISBN 9781921497896 (pbk.)

Includes bibliographical references and index.

Child rearing.
Emotions in infants.
Infants—Development.

649.122

Designed by saso content & design

Typeset in Birka 11/16pt

Illustrations by Simon Goodway

Printed in Singapore by KHL Printing Co Pte Ltd

This book uses paper sourced under ISO 14001 guidelines from well-managed forests and other controlled sources.

The author would like to thank Dr Russ Harris for permission to reproduce the quote from *ACT Made Simple: An easy-to-read primer on Acceptance and Commitment Therapy* (New Harbinger Publications, Oakland, CA, 2009) that appears on page 104.

10 9 8 7 6 5 4 3 2 1

To my little seedlings: Luca, Evie and Sebastian

CONTENTS

Introduction

WHAT DO WE MEAN BY 'BEST START'?

Have you heard the story about the two seedlings sitting on the nursery shelf watching all the people go by?

One seedling says, 'How can you tell the ones who are going to help us grow from the ones who are going to let us wither and die?'

'You can't,' the other seedling replies. 'Our fate is in their hands.'

I can think of more than one occasion when I've bought little seedlings home determined to establish a flourishing garden bed. My intentions have always been nothing less than admirable — adoringly planting them in fresh soil, watering them in and spending at least the next five days tending to them. They grow into wonderful flowers that I love to look at.

But then I forget to water them ... and suddenly the garden is no longer flourishing. The flowers are still there but they're definitely not at their best. Those little seedlings started off with all the potential in the world and then my actions, or rather inaction, sent them in a different direction.

To think of newborn babies like seedlings might be a bit of a stretch, but it's not a bad analogy to keep in mind when thinking of children's foundations. Just like seedlings, babies can't control the conditions they're exposed to. And just like seedlings, babies are born into this world completely dependent on those around them to provide them with what they need in order to grow and develop well. Human babies are born ready to adapt to the environment they're born into — they are 'shaped' by the experiences and interactions they have in their early years.

It is the *quality* of those experiences and interactions that is crucial. Babies can have their basic physical needs met by anyone really, but it is the extra warmth and connection that comes with loving, attentive, sensitive interactions that can make a difference to a baby's foundations. The way a baby is treated during everyday tasks such as feeding, changing, going to sleep, lying on a rug, and just being with their parents all contributes to the way they develop.

It is through these interactions that babies learn about themselves and the world they've been born into. And it is in this way that they develop a framework in which they can place themselves in relation to another person or people — usually their main caregivers — as they grow up. This framework is how they come to 'know' themselves as little people, and it will be used to interpret future interactions and experiences they come across. It's as if they think, 'Well, I'm *this* sort of person so what that person just said to me must mean ...' or 'My experience of people has been *that* so I expect him to ...'

This framework of themselves can be a secure one or an insecure one. It is part of their foundations. These can either develop to be stable and firm, helping to support them through the ups and downs of life, or fragile and prone to crumble under the 'weight' that can come with life as they grow up.

Through their interactions with their caregivers they learn such things as:

- whether they can trust or not

- whether they can feel secure or not

- whether they can be themselves or not

- whether they are valued or not

- whether they can afford to be confident and relaxed or need to be guarded and on alert

- whether they can express emotion or need to suppress it

- whether they will be responded to or whether there is little point in seeking help.

Keeping in mind that babies learn to be a certain way in response to how they are treated, imagine a baby who develops 'a knowing' that they can't depend on their carers, or that they're not valued, or that their feelings don't matter or are not acceptable, or that there's no use in seeking attention to get their needs met. Now consider the possible future of a baby with this start in life, particularly if they continue to be brought up in the same way. What do you think some of their self-beliefs might be? What do you think their self-esteem might be like? What thoughts might they develop about other people? What thoughts and feelings might they develop about themselves? How might they participate in relationships? How might they feel and behave in social situations? How emotionally secure do you think they might feel?

Questions such as these are important to reflect on when it comes to interacting with babies and young children, because their early experiences and interactions provide them with the beginnings of their self-beliefs, thoughts and feelings; of their self-esteem and self-value. They contribute to determining how they operate in relationships; how they behave socially; how they regulate their emotions; their sense of emotional security, and many more important beginnings.

For babies over time to be able to develop trust, to laugh and cry freely, to feel secure and valued and as if they have some control and mastery over their abilities, and to feel confident that they have at least one person they can depend on to help them feel better, they need some simple things. They need us, their parents, to think of them as little beings right from the beginning and be *mindful* that they have needs — the more obvious physical ones as well as the perhaps less obvious emotional ones. They need us to be *attentive* and *responsive* to their needs in a *consistent* way. And they need us to be aware that babyhood is the time when they are learning their very first lessons about themselves, other people, emotions and relationships.

Now imagine a baby developing 'a knowing' that they will be heard, confident that they are valuable enough to be noticed by the most important people in their life; that their feelings matter and will be met with sensitivity; that they can express emotion freely; that they can consistently trust someone will help them when they need it; and that their particular temperament and gene structure will be accepted in all its glory. Think about what has been programmed into a baby with this start to life, their self-beliefs, their sense of value and worthiness, their sense of themselves as a person, their sense of security, their sense of themselves in relation to other people, their ideas about the acceptability of having and expressing emotion, and how they expect to be treated.

This baby is starting life from a position of strength.

This is what is meant by the 'best start': giving babies the type of foundations that are strong enough to allow them to develop and grow into themselves, without being hindered by things like self-doubt, insecurity and difficulty trusting — the sort of psychological cargo that, left unchecked, can potentially throw them off course as they grow up into toddlers, young children, adolescents and adults.

This book is intended to increase awareness about how foundations are formed in babyhood and the power these foundations have over the direction in which children develop emotionally. It will look at how babies' brains are shaped in accordance with how they are interacted with. It will give an insight into what consistency can offer developing babies. It will look at how a child's idea of themselves is created by the ways in which people treat them right from the start. And it will look at why emotional regulation is a vital component of their overall emotional development.

A key focus of this book is us, the caregivers, and how, by being aware of ourselves, we can help our babies receive what they need in order to develop secure foundations, a positive idea of themselves and good emotional beginnings. Scattered throughout are suggestions on how to give babies this strong start to life — those firm foundations.

I certainly don't want to generate guilt in any shape or form. As a fellow parent, I am only too aware of how quick we are to adopt guilt and carry it around on our shoulders all day long. Instead, my aim is to provide information in such a way that it leads you to ask, 'What power does this type of information give me as a parent?'

This book seeks to offer a sense of being 'on the right track' in the wilderness of uncertainty that we wander into as soon as we become parents. And above all else it aims to give a voice to those little babies out there.

Chapter One

HOW THE BRAIN TAKES SHAPE

Babies come into the world with a brain that is open to taking on any shape. It has started to take shape in utero, but it waits to see what environment it's going to have to support its baby through before developing too far. Its eventual shape will be very much influenced by the type of experiences its baby is exposed to as well as the ways people interact with its baby.

By 'shape', I don't mean the external appearance of the brain, as all brains are roughly similar to look at from the outside. By shape, I mean the inside of an individual baby's brain; the network of complicated pathways, connections and structures that make each baby a unique individual. It is the *inside* of the brain that has all the potential in the world to develop in numerous possible directions. But it needs input to know which direction to take.

Why is the brain like this? Basically, the brain needs to be able to help the baby cope in whatever environment they are born into. For example, if a baby is born into a war-torn country experiencing ongoing bombing, and is therefore subject to a huge amount of stress, the brain and the physiological systems it controls, such as the stress response, need to be wired in a way that supports the baby's ability to survive in that environment by adapting to the stress as best as possible. Similarly, if a baby's environment doesn't require their stress system to be super-ready to go, their brain will be wired in a different way with a different set of priorities.

The brain's ability to adapt to different environments is a double-edged sword. On the one hand, it is fantastic, because cultural customs, language, values, beliefs and all manner of life skills can be efficiently incorporated and built on. On the other hand, this same adaptability leaves babies extremely vulnerable if their environment is less than optimal.

Optimal development for each individual baby is what we should all be aiming for, and what shape their brain is in is a key part of their development. In infancy, the brain of a baby is being organised. It goes about forming the neural patterns, pathways and structures that will set the scene for how that baby will operate in their life — how they will behave, think, feel and deal with emotions, to name just a few aspects. It does this through a double act of genes and experience. Currently it is thought that genes play the lesser role, while experience takes the lead in governing how the brain ultimately takes shape. Genes provide the *potential* of a baby and determine certain things like the timing of when a brain part will develop, or the extent to which a particular part is capable of developing as that baby grows. But it is experience that *organises* that baby's potential in a way that will optimise their potential or not.

It's as if the brain comes into the world and says to its baby's environment, 'Right. This is what I have to offer this baby. How can you help me show what I have to offer?' The environment's answer is crucial to that baby.

A baby's environment

Think about what the environment actually is for a baby. It's pretty much their caregivers. Of course, there is their broader environment such as country or city; language; other siblings and extended family members or none; quiet or lots of noise; violence or peace, and the list goes on. But regardless of the make-up of a baby's surroundings, the most important part of the environment for a baby is the person or people who are taking care of them. The experiences and interactions with these people are what matter the most in terms of their emotional and social development.

Why?

Well, babies are born with the basic 'survival' structures and functions. For example, the ability to breathe; and the ability to see, hear, feel, taste and smell sufficiently well so that they can identify what is safe to move towards (soothing sounds, the smell of mother's milk) as well as what they should move away from (pain, loud noises). They come equipped with a basic system that can excrete what their little bodies don't need, a system that gives them rest, and the ability to make a sound (crying) that can gain attention. They have basic reflexes to get food; for example, the crawling reflex at birth to get to the breast, and the rooting and sucking reflexes to get milk. In other words, they are born into the world with the plan to survive and with the basic brain architecture to help this happen.

However, for human babies, survival is more than getting fed, excreting wastes and sleeping. They have been born into the *human* world: survival has to include eventually being able to function effectively in various social environments, because that is what humans do. This, to a large degree, means having the ability to form relationships with other people, to communicate effectively within these relationships, as well as to be self-aware and regulate emotions and behaviour so as to maintain these relationships. Being able to form relationships and function effectively within them is important to being human. It is for this reason that the human brain has specific parts specially assigned to the abilities and systems crucial to forming relationships, such as processing and expressing emotion, and creating and holding emotional memories.

Babies need to be taught how to do this; they can't do it by themselves. As psychoanalyst Donald Winnicott said in his book *The Child, the Family and the Outside World*, '... if you set out to describe a baby, you will find you are describing a baby and someone. A baby cannot exist alone, but is essentially part of a relationship.' Babies need their caregivers to help them. And remember, babies are born with the basic abilities to survive. Being able to connect and form an attachment with another person is part of survival for them.

Just think for a moment how babies might communicate in order to attach to another human being. They have their cry that can differ in pitch and tone, as well as other sounds that can warm the heart; their arms, legs and bodies that can go stiff and rigid in pain or frustration, or snuggly when they feel comfortable, relaxed or safe; their skin that can show redness when distressed; their mouth that can smile to show happiness and pleasure; and their eyes ... oh, their eyes! A baby's eyes can communicate so much, just like ours as adults can. They can be sleepy when tired; wide and alert when looking around at their world; squeezed shut when crying wholeheartedly; or have the 'sick chick' look, as my nanna used to say, when they are unwell. And have you ever watched a baby who is just looking at your face? It's as if those eyes are taking in each and every detail, carefully studying and committing them to memory for later use. And this, to a degree, is exactly what they are doing. Babies are learning to be human through the interactions they have with the people they are around most, and babies actively seek this connection by using all that they have available to them as babies. It's as if they know they are only in their very basic form and need an attachment with an already fully developed member of the species to help them grow and mature.

So the most important part of a baby's environment, regardless of the many forms it may take, is always the other humans in it, especially the key players — the ones closest to them — as these are the people from whom they will learn. The people closest to a baby teach them their very first lessons in everything human, from how to independently feed themselves and go to the toilet, through to how to soothe themselves when distressed, how to feel about themselves, what reactions to expect from other people, how to behave in social situations, and many more. They learn these things by being in a relationship.

Human interaction and brain development

Babies also need an attachment with another human being for their brain to develop in a way that will support them to form relationships with other people. It is *literally* through being in a relationship with another person that their 'relationship-related' brain structures develop. Babies are born with the *potential* to form and function in relationships to whatever level their genes determine, but it is through the *experience* of interacting with their main caregiver(s) that their relationship-related brain parts are organised into a shape that will support them to 'do' relationships well or not as they grow up.

What is fascinating is that young children's brains can actually differ in structure depending on the type and quality of care a child has received right from infancy. An extreme example is the often-referred-to case of 'Genie', a little girl who was severely neglected by her parents from the age of twenty months to thirteen years. From infancy she was tied to a potty chair in a bedroom so she could neither move around nor see outside the room. She was hardly ever attended to by her parents, and if she tried to get their attention to express a need, she would be beaten with a wooden spoon and told to shut up. When Genie was rescued after years of this extreme and chronic abuse, her development was found to be severely delayed: she was unable to talk, she couldn't express emotion in a constructive way and she had virtually no ability to relate to other people. When psychological tests were conducted with Genie to investigate her brain function, she was unable to complete tasks associated with certain parts of her brain, suggesting that these parts had not developed adequately.

A case such as this illustrates just how important human interaction and stimulation are in brain development. Proper development simply doesn't occur in situations of severe deprivation. Genie's case is at the extreme end of the neglect spectrum in that she was deprived of pretty much all stimulation for a prolonged period of time. But it is cases like Genie's that have enabled us to understand that if babies and young children are deprived of positive human interaction over a substantial period of time, the result can be long-term difficulties in not only the cognitive and behavioural domains, but also in social, emotional and relationship abilities, due to the fact that their brains haven't developed as healthily as they could have.

To illustrate this point a little further, we need only look at the Romanian orphans, another often-referred-to group of children when discussing this topic. During the 1980s, Romania suffered severe economic problems and as a consequence more than 65,000 children were placed in orphanages. Most of these children were babies, and because of extremely poor conditions and minimal resources, the children were severely deprived both socially and emotionally. Due to poor staffing levels, infants were left unattended, lying in their cots for up to twenty hours at a time, and thereby receiving an extremely low level of human interaction. When these children were adopted into families in other countries, it was noticed, among other things, that they experienced poor emotional control and social abilities as well as difficulties in forming attachment relationships.

When some of these children's brains were scanned when they were older than six years of age, it was discovered that a major part of the brain that is predominantly assigned to emotional, social and relationship-related abilities was abnormally developed. This finding was consistent throughout the Romanian orphans, in contrast to children who hadn't suffered such social deprivation. Another fascinating discovery was that these deficits were in those children who had spent their infancy and early childhood in the orphanages. The children who were adopted before four months of age, and who therefore received adequate care from a very young age, showed relatively normal development.

Critical and sensitive periods

The findings among the Romanian orphans perfectly illustrate the concept that there are critical and sensitive periods when it comes to brain development. *Critical* periods are times in which the brain *must* receive certain input in order to develop normally. *Sensitive* periods are times in which the brain is *particularly receptive* to certain input in order to develop normally. This means that different parts of the brain are more ready at certain times than at others to receive stimulation so that they can develop to their maximum capacity. So in the case of the

Romanian orphans who had underdeveloped brains, during the time when their brains were ready and waiting to receive adequate human care so that the brain parts assigned to social, emotional and relationship abilities could develop, the orphans didn't receive that input so those brain parts weren't able to develop as they could have. However, the orphans who were adopted at an early age into a loving family probably received adequate input and stimulation at the time the brain was ready for it and so developed normally by comparison.

In the case of Genie, her inability to perform certain tasks in tests associated with different parts of the brain was probably for the same reason. Her severe neglect from infancy to the teenage years meant that she received virtually no stimulation during most of the critical and sensitive periods for the brain to develop adequately. Parts of her brain literally hadn't developed as they should have because when they were ready to develop they didn't receive what they needed.

I'm only bringing up these extreme cases to illustrate just how important interacting with babies is in developing their ability to relate to other people and function socially and emotionally. It's all too easy to take it for granted that babies will develop 'no matter what'. I remember feeling quite shocked by this type of information when I first started to learn about it because I (rather naively, in hindsight) thought that babies have everything in their brain to be grown-ups and do what grown-ups do; they just need those things to grow over time. Learning that parts of the brain need to be stimulated by human interaction in order to develop in an appropriate way has been an eye-opening experience both as a clinical psychologist and as a parent.

In my professional role, when I work with adults with emotional difficulties, this knowledge provides me with a greater understanding of the problems some people experience. If their early history is such that they haven't got the brain structure to support relating well to other people, then maintaining healthy relationships and emotions becomes much harder for them.

In my personal life, this knowledge gives me a fuller understanding of just what I am doing as a parent of young children: I'm literally helping their brains to develop! This realisation has brought forth feelings of pressure, stress and guilt on many occasions when my frustration with my kids has spilled over. But I try to balance these feelings with the knowledge that simply by being in a relationship with my children — one in which, on the whole, I notice them and respond to them in a positively consistent way — I'm going a long way to giving them a healthy emotional brain. Things like smiling regularly, looking at babies warmly, touching them gently, and generally giving them positive interpersonal experiences all set the brain wheels moving in the right direction. And to be brutally honest, I often 'therapise' myself by asking the following question (from Acceptance and Commitment Therapy, or ACT, if you are interested): 'In order to get rid of this pain [feelings of pressure and guilt, etc.], what would I have to stop caring about?' When my answer always comes back as, 'Well, I'd have to stop caring about the impact I'm having on my babies,' that tends to put it all in perspective for me!

When it comes to determining the critical and sensitive periods for the development of social, emotional and relationship-related brain parts, a good rule of thumb is from birth to age three, but it is really an ongoing task. If a baby could talk, he or she would likely say that it is never too early to receive good-quality care and interactions dominated by love, attention and joy. They would also be likely to say that we need to keep it going as they grow. When this occurs the brain parts assigned to forming and functioning in relationships are on their way to being well developed even if the prime time hasn't arrived yet, and will reinforce good patterns as they grow. In general, infancy is a critical period for the parts of the brain that depend on good-quality love and engagement both socially and emotionally.

Below are a few examples of critical and sensitive periods so you can see how they differ.

	Critical	Sensitive
Emotional	0 to 2 years	2 to 5 years
Motor Skills	0 to 2 years	2 to 5 years
Vision	0 to 2 years	2 to 5 years
Early sounds	4 to 8 months	8 months to 5 years
Music	0 to 3 years	3 to 10 years
Thinking	0 to 4 years	4 to 10 years

(Adapted from *Focus on Zero to Three (Part 2) The Brain: Structure and Function*. A CHILD Australia Publication, p. 5., www.childaustralia.org.au/documents/Focus-on-0—-3-Part-2-Brain-Structure-and-Function.aspx)

A way to think about brain development

A baby's brain needs to make the patterns that will be the road maps for that baby as they grow up. And it needs to do this efficiently — at the beginning of a baby's life — so the baby can get on with the job of growing up a certain way in a certain environment. For this reason, the brain is in its most malleable state in infancy up to about age three. It has more potential in these years than it will ever have again. Through experiences and interactions, the brain grows over these years to 80 per cent of the size of an adult's brain. That's pretty amazing when you think about it. Its increase in size is due to the complicated and intricate network of brain cells connecting to form neural pathways in response to the type and quality of experiences its baby is exposed to most regularly.

I think of the Milky Way when I think about the process of brain cells connecting. If you've ever looked up into the night sky you might have seen the Milky Way; it's a galaxy of around 100 billion stars. There are many forms a group of stars could take; however, it is the way these stars are *connected* that creates the shape of the Milky Way. Babies are born with roughly the same number of brain cells as there are stars in the Milky Way and with huge potential for these brain cells to connect. But it is just that at birth: potential. For actual brain cells to connect they need to be stimulated. Brain cells store information and transfer that information to other cells in the brain and body. It is through cells being stimulated that this information gets spread around. In very basic terms, the process works like this. The brain receives input from the environment. Brain cells in the area of the brain related to the type of input fire off information at the same time as other cells that have been stimulated by the same input, and then these cells begin to 'wire' together and make connections. Over time, the connections make neural pathways that will determine how the brain functions across various contexts.

Now the point to really highlight about how the brain develops is that the more regular the experience, the stronger will be the connection between cells and the firmer will be the pathway. It's like when you walk over a patch of grass the same way every day: a path starts to form, and the more the same path is trodden, the more distinct the path becomes.

Equally important is the process called 'pruning'. Pruning refers to the process of 'use it or lose it': brain cells that are not stimulated, and therefore remain unused, will die off. Similarly, if connections and pathways have started to form but are not exposed regularly to the input that caused the connections in the first place, then they too will eventually be pruned, or at least the stronger connections and pathways will dominate.

By brain cells connecting to each other, passing on information and forming neural pathways that become well trodden through regular exposure to the same type of experiences and interactions, a 'story' is created. It's a story about how that particular part of the brain will operate, kind of like an instruction manual.

Alan Fogel, a professor of psychology, says in his book *Infancy: Infant, Family and*

Society, 'Each baby in the first two years of life comes to assess the social world [their environment] as either a safe or a threatening place.' This is done for the baby by their nervous system based on their experiences and interactions with the adults in their environment. So when it comes to the social, emotional and relationship-related parts of the brain, depending on their most prominent and regular experiences and interactions, a baby's instruction manual could read: 'Be open to people; people can be relied upon; it is okay to express how you are feeling; you will get help to soothe upset feelings; it is okay to explore your environment because you have a secure base that is there for you if needed.' Or, it might read: 'Proceed with caution! There is not a lot to feel secure about; people let you down — they are not there when you need them; you can't trust people; BE ALERT TO DANGER AT ALL TIMES!'

Reassuring tip

Often as a new parent feelings of ineptness can visit regularly. The question 'Am I doing this right?' can barge on in many times a day (and perhaps even more often at night). There are times when we can feel so downtrodden and burdened with catastrophic worries that it seems easier to just take to our beds and escape it all. And the thought that we might be creating some type of long-term emotional damage in our babies because of our choices and decisions when it comes to their care is one that can pack a big punch.

In our angst to do 'it' right, it is very easy to get caught up in the offerings of the 'external' world: 'What else can I do/give/buy him to maximise his chances of developing well?' And this is easily reinforced by the competitive playground in which parents often find themselves. It only takes hearing that someone else's child has reached a developmental milestone before our own child to unleash panic that our child might be falling behind. On our own we might be fine with our precious little one not walking yet, but as soon as we hear, or worse yet see, that one of their playmates has reached the walking phase *already*, we can turn on ourselves for not doing enough to encourage them, or scold ourselves for not buying them enough 'aides' to help them develop walking skills. We've just burst through the gates into the competitive playground and started playing the game of comparing. We do it with all good intentions, though; we simply want to help our babies to develop well with all that we have available to us.

But I'd like to reinforce that we, simply as their parents, have a huge amount to offer our babies. In fact, we have something that the external world can never provide: our biological connection to our babies and theirs to us. Sometimes we need a reminder to shift our focus to maximising the potential that connection has to offer.

Just by spending quality time with our babies we are doing great things for their development. Doing simple activities like smiling, singing, talking, cuddling, looking into their eyes, supporting them, comforting them when they are upset, sitting with them, playing, including them, noticing them, enjoying them, being silly with them, saying to them 'I love you' … these are exactly what they need.

We tend to underestimate the impact these types of things can have on babies. When done regularly we are literally helping their little brains to develop and giving them a sense of security in us and in themselves. So if you perhaps find yourself getting stuck in what you aren't doing for your baby, remember that you can do the simple things. And from your baby's perspective, that's doing a lot.

Chapter Two

SAY YES TO CONSISTENCY!

Consistency in the way we respond to and care for our babies is a very important part of giving them the best start we can. It gives them a sense that their world is a predictable one. Now the notion of 'predictability' might sound boring to some of us, but to babies it definitely isn't — it's what they crave. This is because babies are at the phase in their lives when they are learning; virtually everything is new to them. Think for a moment about learning even just one new thing, let alone lots of new things at once. Is it easier to learn if lessons are presented in an unstructured, slap-happy, chaotic manner or if they're presented in a simple, fairly structured, easy-to-follow format? And how does it make you feel when you get to the stage where you can pre-empt what the teacher is going to say or do? Perhaps you feel a bit more confident and a bit calmer as a result? The lessons might become a bit predictable but the by-product of predictability is that you feel secure, 'safe' in the knowledge that you know something. And when you feel safe, you don't need to expend time and energy on trying to find ways to feel calm and peaceful, the feelings we crave when we are uncertain and don't know what on earth to do. Predictability brings a sense of safety and safety brings a sense of calm. For babies, it is a question of which feeling is going to help them best get on with developing and thriving: calm or uncertainty?

A developing sense that the various components of the world around them, and in particular their main caregivers, are predictable and emotionally safe is exactly what is most helpful for babies. We adults are just the same. Whether in our friendships, family relationships or work relationships, predictability and emotional safety can make us feel better. It's no different for our little people.

To clarify things a little further, imagine the following. It's your first day at a new job. You don't have any real thoughts about your workplace yet, you're just happy to settle in and see how it all goes. You are open to learning what you need to in order to perform at your best. The atmosphere is reasonably pleasant — no loud noises or annoying colleagues; a nice view out the window. You have a lovely workspace with good equipment; everything you need to do your job is at your disposal. Your boss has welcomed you warmly and says she is very open to being asked questions and helping you to learn your duties; you find this fantastically reassuring and comforting. You go home after your first day feeling very pleased and confident.

The first few days go swimmingly. Your boss is very approachable and over the past few days you have learned to go to her to seek the guidance needed to do your job. She is always so pleasant and warm — you feel very lucky to have such a great boss! As a result you are thriving and making great progress settling in. At this rate it will take no time at all to learn your new job and work independently. Then, one day, your boss snaps at you for coming to her; she yells at you that she is too busy. You feel a bit confused by her response, but decide she must be having a bad day and do the best you can, fumbling a little without the right information that you really needed from her.

The next day you need to ask her something as no one else in the office knows the answer. After yesterday's dressing down, you approach her a bit tentatively, but you are pleasantly surprised to find she answers your question patiently and warmly. You feel relieved and once again reassured that she is the boss you thought she was. The next time you ask her something she is the same: warm and friendly. You see her in the staff room and she is chatty and pleasant and the next time you need some information from her she offers it openly and kindly.

But the next time you go to her for something, she again expresses frustration and is very rude to you. 'I can't have you coming to me!' she yells. 'Go and learn it yourself and stop harassing me!' she shrieks, red faced. And then she proceeds to mimic you in a high whiney voice, 'Oh, can you answer this? Can you tell me that?' Her eyes bore into you as she finishes with an angry 'Will it ever stop?!'

You feel shocked, upset and very confused. You feel very disillusioned and nervous about approaching your boss again.

You also feel a bit panicky because she is the only one in the office who can give you the information you need. You're not sure how to move forward. You start to doubt yourself and go over and over your interactions with her, searching for where you went wrong. Did you say something to cause the different response from her? Are you doing the wrong thing going to her even though she said you should? Perhaps there is something about you that she just finds distasteful.

These thoughts are going through your mind when you run into her in the toilets. You immediately experience a rush of anxiety as you don't know how she is going to be with you. You look at her tentatively instead of openly as you normally would have. You don't speak out of fear she will be rude again or snap at you. But when she speaks to you, she is once again the pleasant, warm, friendly boss. You feel extremely confused. While you're a little relieved that she seems happy with you again, you can't feel completely comfortable as you have learned that you need to be on your guard with her now. She is a loose cannon, very unpredictable and not emotionally safe to be around. She has taught you that through her interactions with you.

It is very difficult for a relationship that is inconsistent in this way to progress very far. Its capacity to reach genuine deep and meaningful levels is hindered by the need to be constantly on the lookout for signs that it is 'turning to the dark side'. Combine that with the corresponding need to manage the turbulent, uncertain, anxious feelings that come with being around that person and it's enough to give you a headache.

Circumstances permitting, we adults might decide that it is just too much hard work being in such a relationship, and profess to be 'washing our hair' a lot when asked to spend time with such people! For babies, circumstances don't permit. They are locked into a relationship with their main caregivers and have to take it as it is. Babies don't have the option to be physically unavailable. In fact, they don't even have the brain development to know that the relationship isn't a good-quality one — that's 'just the way it is' for them. They don't have the capability to assess a relationship as we do, realise there is better out there, and choose to change to one that is easier and in which their needs are going to be met more.

Babies will, however, adjust to the relationship. We saw in the last chapter that babies are born with the ability to adjust to their environment. But the consequences of adjusting to a less than optimal environment might cause problems for that baby as they get older and need to deal with life. For babies in a relationship in which inconsistent ways of responding and inconsistent ways of caring are dominant, their path of development is regularly being interrupted by tree branches being blown across it. Instead of moving smoothly forward along the developmental path, they are forced to stop and readjust on a regular basis. If babies could articulate the impact of inconsistent care as we can, the stream of thought might be something like this:

'Okay, this is the way it's done. Good. Okay, now I know. I'm starting to feel comfortable. Oh, wait. No it's not, this is the way. Oh, hang on! No it's not. It's the other way. Oh dear. I feel a bit uneasy. Oh wait, no it's not! Is it the other way? Oh, I don't know. Which way is it?!? I don't know what to do or how to respond. I can feel myself getting really worked up and I don't even know how to deal with

that! Should I yell and scream more or should I just shut down altogether? I'm really confused and upset. I want to feel calm and relaxed but I feel agitated most of the time. Sometimes they're nice and give me what I need and sometimes they're not. I've got to try to work out what I am doing wrong because I make them so angry. Who should I go to for help? I keep trying with them but it doesn't feel good to be around them.'

As long as they are caught up in trying to readjust to changing 'rules', their focus cannot be wholly and solely on the job of developing. Instead, they have to combine that job with also adapting to the stress that inconsistency can cause. Inconsistency is stressful for them because, while young babies are capable of a lot of things, they are still only in their very basic form emotionally and physically. Remember that they are born with the basic reflexes, nervous system and abilities to survive. Part of that survival process is to bond with their caregivers — it is crucial for babies to have a connection if they want to survive, learn and function in this human world — so anything that threatens this connection or bond is perceived as stressful by the baby.

Inconsistency in the way a baby is cared for and responded to is a threat to the bond because being on the receiving end of inconsistency teaches a baby that their carer can't be relied on to be there for them. Consistency doesn't so much mean being there 24/7 as it does being consistent in our treatment of our babies as much as possible. For example, it is inconsistent if sometimes you respond to their distressed cries with warmth, nurturing and soothing words and touch, but at other times respond with anger, harsh words and rough handling. A baby's little nervous system is easily overloaded, so unregulated and regular negative treatment is likely to impact on and add to their experience of stress.

Babies need guidance on how to 'be' and function; they don't yet know how to go about a lot of human activities. They need help with things such as how to get soothed; who to go to in order to get fed, comforted, nappy changed; how to play; how to interact with other people; how to deal with feelings that come over them at times; and generally how to be a human and function well. They will continue to need guidance at differing levels of detail throughout their life. And like most of us, babies gain a sense of comfort when they can learn these things in a way that is, to them, simple and smooth rather than chaotic and catastrophic. Consistent ways of responding to them when they are upset, happy, excited, scared or otherwise; consistent ways of handling them and caring for them; consistency in who they are left with — these all contribute to their overall sense of the care they are receiving and of the people providing it.

The gift of consistency

Consistent, sensitive, responsive, warm, empathic care gives babies a sense of security. I think of security as a gift to babies because from a position of security they can go forward and thrive instead of being thwarted by having to learn to deal with the stress that comes with the ups and downs of inconsistent responses and care at such a young age.

From a secure start babies can get on with doing all the things that help them to develop. As they start to move independently, for example, they can explore (as is developmentally appropriate), because they feel reassured that their safe base will be there for them to return to. This is in contrast to a baby who doesn't explore much due to a sense that their base might not be there, a sense they might have developed from being on the receiving end of a range of unpredictable interactions with their carers. Likewise, from a secure position babies can experiment with their voice as they know it will be allowed, or if not then gently curtailed, as opposed to staying silent because they have learned that their experimentations have often led to them being yelled at or met with an angry face or some other type of negative reaction from their carers. As they grow older, they can let their range of emotions come as they will because they can trust that they will be dealt with sensitively, as opposed to tailoring their emotional range mostly to those that have been well received.

When giving care to babies we have to keep outcomes in mind: what outcome are we working towards? And it might help to keep it simple: are we going for a secure or an insecure outcome? While the resounding consensus is most likely 'SECURE!', it is important to state the obvious because the reality is that being a parent can be tough. It is so easy to get caught up in the tangles of our own emotions when we are faced with the more challenging aspects of children's behaviour and emotional expression, and at these times we are more vulnerable to forgetting our long-term goal for our children. Specific strategies to assist with these times will be discussed in Chapter Five, but for now perhaps just get in touch with the difference between feeling secure and insecure, as this kind of reflection can be very useful.

Think about yourself when you feel secure. When we feel secure we can look forward, focus on what we can do and what we want to do, confident that we might actually have a chance of achieving it. The world seems simpler somehow and more within our grasp. Generally we feel more positive; we stand straighter and taller. Perhaps we might do a risky thing like tell a joke to a group of people, or we might have the confidence to stand our ground on something we believe in despite the opinions of the people around us.

Now think about yourself when you feel insecure. When we feel insecure, things don't seem as positive; everything is a little shakier. We probably wouldn't be inclined to tell a joke as we might focus on how it could very well be a fizzer, and it might be easier to just go with the crowd as opposed to standing our ground, despite what we believe. We might not even have well-formed strong beliefs in the first place and instead have become used to looking to others and adopting their beliefs and opinions about things. We might not extend ourselves too far in our career or relationships, as we might not have a sense that anything good could come of it.

A feeling of security as they grow is what we are ideally after for our children in our parenting of them. Of course, there are other factors aside from our parenting that can cause our kids to feel shaky, under-confident and insecure at times as they grow into little people, but giving them a *core* sense of security and a confidence that they can count on the main adults in their life can only help them as they come across the various bumps they will need to ride. And there will be bumps: those that their personality might set them up for, those that come with interacting with other little personalities they come across, or those that come with learning new concepts when they get to school. But a genuine sense of security will give them protection of sorts. While it won't prevent them from experiencing the ups and downs of life, it will likely buffer the impact for them, especially if we continue to offer the same type of communication and care that has fostered that sense of security in them right from babyhood.

I think of kids with a core sense of security as having a couple of pieces of bubble wrap tied firmly around them. When they bump into the unpleasant parts of their little lives, emotional or otherwise, they will still feel the associated upset, but the impact might not be as harsh as it might be without the bubble wrap of security.

It's important to remember that simply by being consistent in how we care for and respond to our babies we can make a huge difference to their perception of their world. Babies operate by 'getting a sense' of something. Consistency in the way they are cared for in everyday activities and responded to can contribute to them getting a sense that they are in a safe, comfortable and secure place. Ongoing inconsistency can give them a sense that they are in a place that is unstable with no rhyme or reason to feel safe or secure. It might seem small to us but from a baby's point of view consistency is as important to their emotional development as eating healthily is to their physical development.

Why else is consistency so important?

Consistency is like a language that the brain understands in order to develop in a well-organised way. Remember that the brain develops via the process of different brain cells being stimulated by input received from the environment; for example, a primary carer's facial expressions, touch, words and speech. Over time, the brain cells connect together to form neural pathways that are congruent with the type of input that is presented the most. The more regular the experience, the stronger will be the connection between cells and the firmer will be the pathway. The more regular, repeated and consistent the input or experience, the stronger the brain architecture will be, and it is the brain architecture that will support the way a baby develops. So for a baby to develop healthily, they need the input to not only be appropriate — gentle facial expressions, affectionate touch and soothing words and speech — but also be proffered in a consistent way as it makes the brain's job easier to create healthy, strong structure more smoothly and efficiently.

The type of care determines the quality: healthy or not so healthy. How that care is presented determines the strength of the supporting architecture: strong or not so strong. From a baby's point of view, the optimum combination is healthy quality supported by a strong, secure structure. This way they can have the best chance of developing as they were born to.

From the baby's point of view

This is what parenting is all about — it needs to be done from the baby's point of view. We don't bring up children for us; we bring up children for them. While this might be self-evident and rather obvious, it can be easy to forget at times. It is easy to assume they know how to do things like manage their frustration or organise their thoughts in a way that will lead to logical and sensible results, especially as they get older and appear more grown up. But from a baby's point of view everything is new: they need to be taught, and what is presented to them most — in verbal and non-verbal format — becomes what is normal and most familiar. Importantly, that applies whether what is being presented is helpful or unhelpful to their development.

A term that is referred to often in child development and parenting is 'secure attachment'. This refers not to the parents' relationship with their child, but to the child's relationship with their parents. Once again, it is all about the child's viewpoint and whether, *to them*, their relationship with their parents or main caregivers is secure or insecure. Having our babies develop a secure attachment to us is the aim of the game; this is the gold standard. When a baby has a secure attachment, their needs are being met and they are on the way to developing that healthy core sense of security that will help them along their path in life.

When thinking of attachment, I always visualise babies sitting back with a discerning look on their face, assessing their parents on how well they are performing in their job as parent — kind of like a performance appraisal.

We have a set of KPIs, or Key Performance Indicators, against which we are measured. If we are assessed as performing to a

certain standard on most of the points, we are doing well. If not, then there might be consequences. The thing is, though, that when it comes to being measured in terms of how well we are helping our babies feel securely attached to us, the consequences also affect them. This is great if we do a good job, but not so good if we don't. Secure attachment sets babies up with a healthy, robust, well-functioning 'inside guide' who has a good chance of feeling eager about life and learning, who can trust, and who has a good ability to care about, love and have empathy for others. Insecure attachment can lead to a different path, one that is travelled by a 'fragile guide' who is prone to confusion, has a poor sense of self and possible difficulties feeling and relating to other people throughout life.

And as I am writing this, I can feel the guilt threatening to stomp all over me.

So what I desperately want to include at this stage is an acknowledgement of the guilt and emotional pressure that talk of secure attachment can bring. I, as a parent of young children, am very familiar with the feeling of guilt — it swirls around me often. So I, as a parent and a professional interested in the mental health of mothers and babies, cling onto the notion of the 'good enough mother' proposed by psychoanalyst Donald Winnicott. In his concept of the 'good enough mother', Winnicott acknowledged that the needs of a baby can be met by the 'ordinary devoted mother'; by 'the ordinary mother in her ordinary loving care of her own baby'. The point that I think is most important to emphasise is that it is the 'ordinary' care that naturally follows 'devotion' to a baby that will do the job for that baby. It is not the idea that some type of 'perfection' has to be present for a baby to get what is needed to feel comfortable, safe, secure and bonded. From a baby's point of view, *ordinary* devotion is enough; perfection is not necessary.

It is we who get caught up in the idea of being perfect, and particularly the consequences of not being perfect or providing perfect care to our babies (from our own perspective, I might add). Health professionals certainly don't expect perfection from mothers in parenting their babies. Babies don't expect perfection — they are happy with the simple things. If we keep in mind that it is the perspective of the babies that matters most, then we might shift away from the thought that we need to be satisfying some type of perfection criteria, because babies don't expect us to be perfect, we do.

Winnicott also made reference to a 'not good enough' mother/carer. By this descriptor he encapsulates the sort of behaviour that leads to creating a sense of insecurity in babies. So from the babies' point of view their care would seem unpredictable; their important needs would be met sometimes but often not; care would perhaps be given but then taken away; and generally there would be no rhyme or reason to their environment. Neglect and abuse would fall into this category as well, of course.

In light of this, it might be of interest to know that it has been established that the two main things that are most important in steering babies onto the track of security, as opposed to the bumpy road of insecurity, are the *quality* and the *responsiveness* of the interaction with babies. So given that an 'ordinary mother' usually has a lot to do in this hectic world of juggling roles and managing several tasks at once, to be reassured that we are being 'good enough', it might be helpful to keep in mind the key things that will help our babies and children feel securely attached to us. Perhaps take note of the words: 'LOVING', 'DEVOTED', 'QUALITY' and 'RESPONSIVE', and 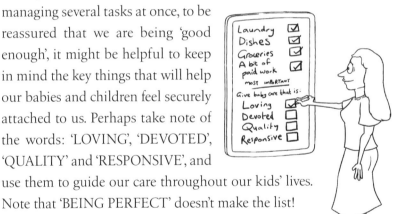 use them to guide our care throughout our kids' lives. Note that 'BEING PERFECT' doesn't make the list!

Sometimes it has to be about the parent as well as the child

Parenthood can be thought of like a job. I don't, however, mean for this statement to generate feelings of foreboding and drudgery. In saying 'parenthood is like a job', I mean it is something that we are *actively doing*; what we do has an effect. We are creating and building. We are given some materials to work with: a little body with bones, muscles, organs and a brain ready to develop, a set of genes, natural personality traits and a nervous system set up to feel stressed a lot or a little. The job is to create and build a well-functioning person to co-exist with other people in a quality way. We do this by moulding the materials we've been given to the best of our and their ability. Our tools are simple: our facial expressions, tone of voice, touch, our ability to provide affection and comfort, and our ability to be still and observe so that over time we can develop an ability to tune in to what our babies need and then meet their needs with sensitivity.

Building and creating require one eye to always be on the outcome, what we are working towards. Regularly checking in by asking the question, 'Are we still on track?' is a necessary part of maintaining focus.

But maintaining a focus on how we want our children to be in terms of emotional and other development and actually doing the job of helping them achieve it can be two very different things. Sometimes it is quite easy to have the focus, but a lot more difficult to put in the effort required. This is probably because we are human. When the tools to do the job are predominantly us, the tools get tired.

When most tools are used constantly they need to be serviced. They need this care and attention to maintain a certain quality. A parent's tools need the same type of servicing to maintain their quality as well.

At the risk of sounding clichéd, it is vitally important that parents give themselves some care and attention. As far as our babies are concerned, it is the long-term outcomes that are most important. They might prefer *not* to have us around for an hour or two if that means they can have a more relaxed, calm parent interacting with them most of the time. Logistically, it is not always easy to achieve this 'servicing', but if the opportunity is there and guilt about leaving your child is the main obstacle in the way, perhaps it might be useful to think about things from your baby's point of view. What is the quality of the tools from their perspective? Are they working well or malfunctioning regularly? Is it best to step out briefly or keep using them in their current state?

Circumstances permitting, it has to be okay to take a brief time out. When we become parents we go through a lot of emotional changes that we aren't necessarily prepared for, nor expecting. It is common for parental attention and focus to genuinely shift away from the self and onto the baby. Perspective changes and life and certain pursuits followed before baby can seem selfish and frivolous once baby is here. All we want to do is protect and take care of this precious little being we are so blessed to have. And this is absolutely necessary; newborn babies and children *need* their parents to be there for them. They rightfully deserve to be the number one priority.

But it is important to remember that from where our babies are lying, the job of bringing them up in an environment in which they feel safe, loved, valued and secure can be done by the ordinary devoted mother/parent/carer — the 'good enough mother' (or father). That is, *ordinary* not *super*-ordinary. When we become parents we don't suddenly develop superhuman powers that allow us to shut down our need to shower regularly, to sleep, to require interaction with other adults, to enjoy having our hair done, to exercise, to just sit and think — and perhaps bigger needs like working and spending time with our partners.

Even as I write these words I feel a conflict within me: the psychologist versus the mother. The psychologist is seeing reason but the mother in me is asking, 'Doesn't having a genuine want to still do these things mean that I am less of a mother somehow?' And as a mother, this question doesn't seem all that irrational. So it's important to step back and reframe a bit. Instead of assuming that wanting to have our basic needs met is a bad thing, think about what we are trying to give our babies when we meet their basic needs. In them it creates, among other things, a sense of calm and from this position they can get on with the job of growing up to reach their potential. It's the same for us. If we can get our basic needs met — and these are different for every parent — we have a greater chance of feeling calmer, less stressed and more energised. From this position we can get on with the job of bringing up our babies to the very best of our ability.

Genuinely wanting to do things *other* than take care of our babies doesn't mean we are bad, or 'less' in any way. It doesn't equate with being a 'not good enough' parent. It simply reinforces that we are human. It might be helpful to have an active 'balance radar', regularly checking in with what we need to do to give our babies devoted care, and what we need to do for us to feel we can provide this care in a quality way. Each parent is different and comes into the role of parent with a different set of personality traits, expectations, family history and personal circumstances. It can take a bit of time and thought to work out what we are capable of including in our life in addition to being devoted to our babies.

Keeping it simple is always helpful. Having the basic needs of babies in mind and quickly running through them when we need to make decisions about what and how much 'extra' we do in life might also be useful. First though, we have to accept that it will take time for us to learn exactly what our babies' needs are, what the KPIs are that we need to meet in order for our babies to develop secure attachment. It takes time to accurately read cues. Most parents haven't had a lot of practice at understanding what babies need. Do they need food, their nappy changed, soothing or some other elusive action that is beyond our knowledge at the time? Who knows? It is hard to tell at first. So there is a need to be patient in order to develop the ability to interpret the signals and cues.

Here are a few valuable tips to guide you:

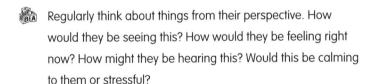 Regularly think about things from their perspective. How would they be seeing this? How would they be feeling right now? How might they be hearing this? Would this be calming to them or stressful?

Be still and observe. What do the sounds and movements of *my* baby mean? What are they trying to communicate?

Try to develop the ability to 'tune in' to them and what they need physically and emotionally as much as possible. What might they need?

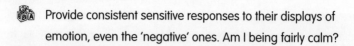 Provide consistent sensitive responses to their displays of emotion, even the 'negative' ones. Am I being fairly calm?

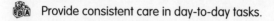 Provide consistent care in day-to-day tasks.

If you need to go out, leave them with someone they are familiar with.

Provide regular affectionate, gentle touch — lots of cuddles.

Regular use of soothing, gentle words and speech provides comfort.

Remember facial expressions convey a lot. Look into their eyes. What is my expression saying?

Spend time with them and play — be at their level.

Remember the words LOVING, DEVOTED, QUALITY and RESPONSIVE when interacting with them.

Something to keep in mind

The feeling of guilt can intrude too much in parenting and leave us feeling unnecessarily bad too often. By keeping in mind that, from the baby's point of view, it is the simple things that come from ordinary devoted care that help them to feel secure in their relationship, you will hopefully keep the guilt at bay a little bit. Perhaps reflect on the following simple rhyme every now and then to keep the important, yet simple, points in mind.

Ode to Mum and Dad

I'm your precious little baby
You are my mum and dad
I know you do everything for me
And for that I'm very glad.

I learn from you every day
In everything you do
From the way you soothe my cries
To the way you clean up my poo!

When your care of me gets predictable
In your warm and special way
I actually really love it
Because I feel safer by the day.

I love when you give me cuddles
And when you kiss my feet and nose
It makes me feel warm and loved
Gee, I'm glad it's you two I chose.

When you soothe me when I hurt
When you tell me it's okay
I learn that I can count on you
To ease my pain away.

When you watch me very closely
As I explore my world and play
I learn that I can depend on you
To be there either way.

As you gently stroke my hair
When I'm trying to go to sleep
I'm really getting a sense
Your heart is mine to keep.

My safety and security
Is what will help me grow
It really means a lot to me
That this you make efforts to know.

To me you are the only people
On the whole entire earth
And from your eyes, your voice, your touch on me
I always know my worth.

So Mum and Dad, my parents
You have given the best ever gift to me —
A sense of being secure and loved
Now I can be the person I was born to be!

Chapter Three

DEVELOPING YOUR CHILD'S SENSE OF SELF

As Dr Seuss said, 'A person's a person, no matter how small.' For a baby to begin to develop a sense of self that is robust and healthy, it is essential to keep in mind the wisdom of that line.

'Self-concept', or the idea a person has of themselves, starts in babyhood. It develops with the baby and according to what they are developmentally capable of. So it starts in basic form and increases in complexity and structure as a baby moves into being able to speak, and to use and understand words in relation to themselves.

Self-concept can't form in isolation from other people. It forms *because* of other people. The way a person views themselves is very much influenced by the way people have interacted with them throughout their life — babyhood included. In fact, babyhood and early childhood are extremely important when it comes to self-concept and self-esteem. It is in these life periods that we are biologically primed to take on and incorporate a set of core self-beliefs. This is discussed further in Chapter Five.

Our self-beliefs are like core 'truths' about ourselves and who we are as a person. They are very important to the way in which self-esteem progresses, because the way we learn to look at ourselves is the way we will *assume* other people look at us. For example, if a person believes she is hopeless and disgusting, she will *assume* other people see her as hopeless and disgusting. And why not? If this is the 'truth' about her, then of course that is how others will perceive her.

Our core self-beliefs are like looking glasses. We put them on and it is through them that we view ourselves and the world around us. It is through the lenses of our core self-beliefs that we interpret the looks that people give us, the words they choose to communicate something to us, and their behaviour towards us. It is through this process of interpreting based on the nature of our beliefs that the core beliefs are reinforced over and over again. The stronger they get, the more power they can have over our lives too. Let's look again at the above example of the woman who truly believes she is hopeless and disgusting, and assumes other people see her that way too. Think about the possible consequences for that woman. She might not be too keen on applying herself academically in order to widen her job options. After all, what's the point? She's too hopeless. She might not want to go out and form good-quality relationships that could enrich her life. How could she? She's too disgusting.

Left unchecked or unchallenged, our core self-beliefs have the potential to set the course of our life. By the time people realise that they might need to challenge their core self-beliefs, they are so deeply entrenched that it is often quite a difficult task to shift away from them and make new, healthier ones. It would be much easier to have healthier ones to begin with.

How does self-concept form?

Babies are capable of sensing what being picked up roughly feels like as opposed to what it feels like to be picked up lovingly and warmly. They are capable of developing a sense for what an angry tone of voice sounds like as opposed to a soft, soothing tone. When their vision becomes clearer they are capable of 'reading' faces. They can tell the difference between a happy, loving expression and expressions of anger and disgust, for example. They aren't able to name these emotions using words — they just aren't up to that developmentally yet — but they can get a feel for the different touches, tones and expressions as well as the amount of warmth (a lot or not much) that goes with them. For example, if a crying baby is met with an angry face and irritated tone of voice, and roughly picked up and patted heavily on the back on a regular basis, then that baby will develop feelings about that. Conversely, if a crying baby is met with a sympathetic face with kind eyes and a soothing voice, and picked up gently and cuddled closely, then a 'feeling state' would develop that accorded with that treatment.

Self-concept starts at this level, as feeling states become associated with images of their main caregivers relating to them. As babies develop and grow, they learn that certain images come with certain feeling states: a warm smile brings about a comfortable feeling; an irritated grimace elicits an uncomfortable feeling. They start off with the ability to experience moments of this image–feeling state association. Babies don't have the ability to have a sense of 'all the time'; it's as if they experience still photographs of how people are with them instead of a flowing movie. As they get older, they develop the ability to store images in memory. If the moments are repeated, more emotion is invested into the repeated interactions their caregivers have with them and patterns start to emerge. They start to get more of a flowing self-knowledge, a sense or 'knowing' about themselves in relation to other people. This sense of self takes shape through the way in which they are treated from the start, and the shape is made by all the moments that are similar being put together. If the moments are mostly warm, responsive, loving ones then the sense of self shapes up along the lines of: 'I'm valuable and loveable and I'm growing more certain of this by the day.' If the moments are the opposite — rather cold, unresponsive or inconsistent and not very loving — then the sense of self is more susceptible to being: 'I'm not very valuable; there is nothing about me that is worthwhile or loveable; there's something generally negative about me.'

So it is the interactions that occur repetitively or most often that are important. As I discussed in Chapter One, neural pathways are formed by repetition. Because of this process, the repeated caregiver–baby interactions set a baby's expectations of other people and help them predict how they will be treated: whether they are in for a pleasant or unpleasant experience, for example.

From caregivers behaving in similar ways each time they interact with babies during day-to-day activities, babies can learn about how things and people in the world operate. It is through being on the receiving end of repeated interactions with their caregiver that they learn about themselves, and the quality of the interactions determines whether they get a sense that they are something positive or something negative.

Babies are extraordinary interpreters of communication right from the start. However, they are better able to understand the *way* something is communicated than *what* is communicated. Remember, they are born with a basic nervous system that enables them to assess whether something is safe or unsafe. When they are younger, babies best understand communication not through *what* is said but by *how* it is said and by the way they are handled. If a baby's cries for help are most often met with a facial expression, body language, tone of voice and treatment that all says, 'I love you and I'm here to help you,' then that's the feeling state ('safe') that the baby understands and downloads in regard to expressing needs. That warm response is what they will expect when they cry for help. However, if the facial expression, body language, voice tone and treatment most often says, 'You are annoying and I resent doing this,' then that is the feeling state ('unsafe') they will download and they will learn to expect an irritated response when they cry.

The first baby is starting to develop a sense of self that says, 'I am loved and am worthy of attention and help — I feel safe.' The second baby's sense of self has started off as, 'I am annoying and a bother — I feel uncertain and unsafe.' The first baby will learn to predict that by crying they will receive a warm response from their caregiver; and that nice (safe) feeling is reinforced each time that experience occurs. They are learning and internalising that when they ask for help they get it and it's offered without a problem. They learn that it is safe to ask. The second baby will learn to predict that when they cry they will be met with a lack of warmth and abrupt treatment which gives them a not very nice (unsafe) feeling and *that* is what is reinforced each time that experience occurs for them. This baby is learning and internalising that when they ask for help it doesn't go down too well. They learn that it is not that safe to ask.

Babies obviously can't use the words 'loved', 'warm', 'annoying', 'safe' and 'unsafe' to categorise how they feel, but they get the general sense of them and how this makes their body feel. This sense is stored away and will eventually underpin their expectations of other people as they grow up — 'I expect negative reactions from people'; 'I expect positive reactions from people', for example. It will give them their idea of how they are as a person in relation to other people and how other people feel about them — 'I am loveable'; 'I am annoying', for example. This is how their self-concept starts to form. They develop a sense that their 'self' is either a 'good concept' or a 'not so good concept'. It's as if they adopt their treatment and develop their idea of themselves based on its quality.

It's through us noticing them — when they need comfort, help, to play — and letting them know through our touch, facial expression, voice and general behaviour that we have noticed and that we are available to them, that we start to set the background of how they will think and feel and what they will believe about themselves. It's as if we are starting to build the glasses through which they will see themselves. We begin the manufacturing process with our non-verbal behaviour and our words add to the process as they get older and move further along the developmental path.

When words are added to their self-concept

As babies grow into toddlers and young children they develop the ability to speak and can now start to understand some of the words that accompany the facial expressions, body language, tone of voice and treatment of their caregivers. And again, if these words are used repetitively, they will be incorporated into their understanding of themselves. Combined with the continued non-verbal communication, they can eventually learn their 'descriptors' (the words that describe themselves). Word combinations like: 'you are a thoughtful girl'; 'you are a beautiful person'; 'you put in your best effort'. Or word combinations like: 'you are a whinger'; 'you aren't normal like other kids'; 'you always ruin things'. When words are added to the mix, their lessons become clearer. What makes them 'them' becomes a combination of mainly strengths or a combination of mainly faults.

This emerging sense of themselves, that started with images and feeling states that over time developed into patterns and now underpins what they expect from other people, becomes even fuller and more detailed with words that they can use to describe themselves. For a young child with a self-concept that is on the more robust, positive side, it might go something like: 'I have a sense that I am a valuable, loveable person and know I am thoughtful, do my best and am a beautiful person ['cause my parents tell me].' For a child with a self-concept that is a little less positive, it might go: 'I have a sense that I am annoying and irritating and I know that I am a whinger, not normal like other kids and I always ruin things ['cause my parents tell me].'

This is the idea they carry of themselves as their social world opens up a bit more and they start to interact with a wider range of people, thereby coming across various situations they haven't come across before. Their sense of themselves is always in the background coming into play when they have to interpret and understand various things that happen around them. It is put up as an explanation for why 'David didn't invite me to the party', or why 'Mum gave my sister a toy and not me' or why 'Santa gave me socks and undies instead of a bike'. It's because, 'I'm annoying/a whinger/not normal ... of course.'

Young children, no matter how positive or robust their self-concept is, don't have the ability to understand and cope with the complex social dynamics presented in the above scenarios without the help and guidance of an attuned caregiver, but the ones with the more positive idea of themselves are in a much better position to work through them. This is mainly because, in order to have a positive self-concept in the first place, they have caregivers who have, right from the beginning, thought of them as being a 'good concept'. And just like in the business world, the good concepts are the ones that have all the resources, time and energy poured into them.

As discussed in Chapter One, a child's set of genes and natural personality traits also contribute to how a child functions in the world, but the way they are interacted with organises these genes and traits to head in a certain direction. The children with positive self-concepts, and all children for that matter, will obviously vary in how they react to various situations they come across because there are so many variables involved, but the necessary work has been put into these children to foster a genuine sense of security and a certainty that they are inherently good little people. So while they might experience dents here and there, they are secure in the knowledge that they have qualities that make them likeable and acceptable, and that they have caregivers who are available to support them and who can help them when they need help (because they have always been there for them when needed in the past). These are the things that can make a huge difference when our little people start to take their sense of themselves out into the big, wide world.

So it would be giving our kids a really good present if we installed in them a positive, robust, strong sense of themselves as valuable individuals.

This would be a gift that keeps on giving because the ultimate aim of parenting is to bring up children to be independent — to be able to go out into the world, to function well

and ideally have a good shot at reaching their individual potential. A person who has a genuine sense that they are inherently a good person, and that they have worthwhile abilities that can be used to have a go at achieving what they want in life, is in a better position than a person whose sense of self is more on the negative, shaky, under-confident side. The first person is more likely to see their potential and head off towards it. It's as if they are 'the captain' of their life. They are in a position to see the possible directions they could take, make the decisions about which to take and then confidently 'steer the ship' toward their choices. The second person might be more like 'the crew' taking instructions from 'Captain Limitation', who constantly reminds them of the restrictions their negative self-beliefs and poor self-concept put on their life.

It would be nice for our kids to have a strong sense of self as they grow up — to be the captain of their life.

LIFE'S POSSIBLE DIRECTIONS

So to continue the Dr Seuss theme that opened this chapter, here's some more wise advice for our kids as they grow into their age-appropriate independence:

'You have brains in your head. You have feet in your shoes. You can steer yourself any direction you choose. You're on your own. And you know what you know. And YOU are the one who'll decide where to go …'

As they get a little older

As our children get older their sense of self can take a battering. When they start to mix with other children for lengths of time — at preschool and then school, for example — they can experience episodes of self-doubt. This is the time in their life when they are introduced to the gem, 'You're not my friend anymore!' and others like, 'You're dumb,' 'You're fat,' 'No one likes you,' 'You can't read/draw/write/speak/run/play soccer/dance/make paper aeroplanes as good as me.' It might be one of the first times that they have to question themselves because they see that there are other children who are similar to them — 'He's good at colouring-in too, but I thought I was the best at colouring-in!' — and different to them — 'He can tie his shoelaces; I can't.' The way they do things is suddenly receiving different reactions, sometimes positive and sometimes not so positive.

It's as if their 'self-story' — about how to think, behave and feel — gets reviewed and revised. It doesn't necessarily change but it can be modified as it receives new and different input on a regular basis as they continue to mix with other children and adults through the process of growing older.

This is a time to be there for them, and to check in now and again with how they are travelling emotionally. And being there for them means understanding that from several different sources they are receiving messages that they are good at some things and not good at others, that they are well behaved and not well behaved, that they are included and not included, liked and not liked — and they are trying to cope with these messages the best way they can with still developing cognitive abilities.

The way they cope can vary; it is not unusual for them to feel left out and different to other children on occasion as a result of being at the receiving end of negative messages. Left unchecked these experiences of feeling different can potentially skew their view of themselves in a negative direction, especially if they occur often and are not balanced out with other more positive information about them.

Some ways to help

Just as noticing their strengths and letting them know through our actions and words that we have noticed is helpful to our kids developing and maintaining a positive sense of themselves, noticing when they are vulnerable and supporting them through these times is equally helpful.

When thinking about how to help kids feel better when they are feeling vulnerable and different from the other kids, I think of Mumble, the fluffy, blue-eyed dancing penguin living among the sleek, black-winged singing penguins in the movie *Happy Feet*. Little Mumble's difference put him on the periphery of his peers and caused his dad to have awkward, stilted penguin-interactions with him. But if we didn't focus on how he was different, we saw that Mumble was loyal, fun, free-spirited, strong of character and determined. While he was affected by being left out, he also came across as having an 'Oh well, let's get on with it' attitude. He had a surprisingly sound sense of himself given he was the only one in the entire penguin community who couldn't sing and who received regular 'he's not like us; there's something wrong with him' messages.

I like to think that he was all these things because of his mum (combined with his own personality). To my eyes, Mumble's mum was his resilience until he was able to do it for himself. She focused on his strengths rather than his difference, accepted him as he was, and this helped him to do it too. She wasn't judgemental or critical of him; she didn't see him as 'faulty'. By focusing on his strengths and supporting him through his vulnerable times, she gave his developing sense of self a bit more of a balanced view. He learned he was more than 'just different'. I'd like to offer that this is what we can do with our kids to help them maintain a more positive sense of self when they are faced with messages that try to tell them otherwise. Simple things like:

- Keeping in mind that they need to develop a balanced view of themselves and that it might only be us, their parents, who can offer this view at times.

- Being their strengths 'coach' — reminding them that they have other qualities on board; that there are components to them other than those that make them feel separate from the people who are coaching for the 'different' team.

- Helping them to expand their view to consider that sometimes being left out or feeling that they don't fit in could be due to mismatched strengths rather than an inadequacy on their part; for example, being really good at art but hanging around kids who play soccer.

- Normalising vulnerability and accepting it — thereby helping them to see that all children have things that make them different too, and this puts them all in the same basket in a sense.

Listening to what they have to say about their day and then re-wording or re-framing the day's events for them, thereby helping them to focus on different parts of the story (and on different parts of themselves).

 Perhaps remembering that when they are feeling different, a bit emotionally unsafe or at least on shaky ground, a cuddle and something that reassures them that they are safe with us might also be in order.

 Making an extra effort when they've had a rough day to do a family activity that helps them to remember they have another group of people who will always accept them, and who hold their developing sense of self high on the priority list.

Chapter Four

EMOTIONAL REGULATION AND THE IMPORTANCE OF SELF-AWARENESS

Recently my three-year-old daughter dropped and smashed my watch. A bit of background:

This was my third watch — the previous two had been damaged ...

I had said many times, 'Please leave my watch and other things on my bench alone.'

It had been a long time between watches — I'd only bought it two weeks ago.

I really liked this watch.

So this is how it went: I came out of the en suite and my daughter was still in there. I heard a tinny thud and a small smash and knew instantly that my watch had (again) been broken. I yelled out, 'NOOOOO!!!' and rushed to the bathroom to see my daughter's chubby little toddler hand fly behind her back and my watch placed back on the bench, face down. I turned the watch over to see the glass had cracked and smashed. So I yelled, in what in hindsight was a rather whiny way, 'My watch is broken! Oh no! I loved this watch! [All of this amplified by my being in the bathroom.] Now I don't have a watch again!' and stomped out and sat on the bed where I continued my rant. 'Why can't I have anything that stays good and unbroken? [Thinking of my make-up that has on occasion mysteriously disappeared or been rubbed all over something.] Aaaaarrgh!!'

My daughter was in a flurry. She started to come towards me and then went back to the watch, then back towards me. Reaching out her pyjama-clad arms she said in a worried voice, 'Mummy?' At this point my husband and son were heard coming up the stairs to see what all the commotion was about. My daughter scurried away, long hair flying, into the wardrobe.

I was aware she was feeling extremely worried and probably scared, but I continued to let my emotion flow to my husband. 'My watch is broken. I only had it for two weeks. Now I don't have a watch again. I can't keep anything good!' Blah, blah, blah …

My husband looked at my daughter now hiding under the chair and said in his calm voice, 'You've broken Mummy's watch and she is very sad and angry. Look at her face — look how sad she is.' She came out and tentatively looked at me sitting on the bed with my head in my hands. 'You need to go to Mummy and help fix her feelings,' he continued. At this, my little three-foot three-year-old shuffled over to me in her pink flannelette pyjamas, arms extended and face crumbling into a cry, and said through her tears, 'I sorry I bwoke your watch,' and put her arms around me.

Now this is where I will pause, as I see this spot in the 'real-life drama' as the fork in the road in terms of how we react to our kids when we are really emotionally worked up — which can happen often in parenting. This is the spot when our own ability to manage our emotions is truly tested. Can I put the brakes on or are my brakes not strong enough to slow down the surge of emotions when in full swing? Will being immersed in my strong emotion take me away from my ability to stop myself? Will it make me blind to my daughter's needs at that time? Will I get stuck in this state of ranting and raving for longer than is necessary? And if I do, what could be the consequences for my precious girl? Important questions to ask.

The way I choose to react to my daughter in this situation will have an effect on her, especially if the way I react is always the same in similar situations, past and future. The way I react and deal with my strong emotions is teaching her about emotional regulation, or how to manage her emotions. It teaches her firstly a 'model' of how it is done — how emotions are shown and handled — that she can incorporate and adopt to use among other people; and secondly, whether her nervous system needs to stay on high alert or whether it can learn to settle down after experiencing highly charged feelings; whether she will, over time, learn and internalise effective strategies to calm herself or not.

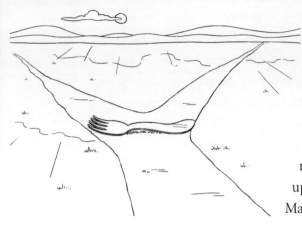

So we are at a fork in the road.

The avenue to the left of the fork is: Continue to rant and rave, letting my anger work me up more and more. Make my voice louder, my actions more abrupt, perhaps slam some things down; tell her how stupid she was to break it; how I TOLD her NOT TO TOUCH IT IN THE FIRST PLACE! Send her to her room and to go to bed. Not discuss it again or maybe bring it up again when something else happens.

What this reaction would require of me: To give in to my anger; let it dominate. To ignore my daughter's cries; her attempts to say she is sorry; her attempts to reach out to me to comfort me, to 'fix' my feelings; to ignore her attempts to enlist my help to make her feel better, to help her calm down. Also to ignore the fact that she is three years old. Ignore the fact that she didn't do it on purpose, that it was an accident, that she is very remorseful and that she is trying to 'repair' the situation — which is actually a very adaptive way of handling it. And also to ignore the fact that I left the watch within her reach in the first place.

What this reaction would require of her: To have that worried, distressed feeling continue to go un-soothed. To see her attempts at trying to say sorry and fix the situation be dismissed and not valued. To feel lost as to how to fix the situation; lost as to how to calm herself down. To see the person she goes to for help not help her to feel better. To feel very confused and scared. To have her side of the story — that it was an accident — go unheard. Perhaps to retreat, withdraw from this person who is frightening her. To go to bed with a feeling that she is a 'bad' girl.

The consequences: Well if this was a once-off incident, there would probably be minimal consequences for my daughter. However, if this was the way most incidents of a similar nature were handled, then some of the consequences could be:

- A general wariness around me.

- A growing sense of confusion about her relationship with me.

- She might learn to not come to me when she made a mistake out of fear of getting into trouble and therefore not get the help she needs at that time.

- A sense that she can't rely on me to soothe her. She would have to develop her own ways of soothing which might be okay or might be maladaptive behaviours.

- A growing sense that she is in some way 'bad' or that she causes problems. This might develop into a core belief she has about herself that might continue into adulthood.

- She might internalise my reactions as 'the way' to react when someone does something that makes her feel angry. She might start to behave in the same way and never really learn ways to get out of that state of intense emotion/explosive behaviour cycle (because she has never been taught ways to get out of it if only shown the cycle). Her nervous system might stay on high alert longer than it needs to and won't develop ways to effectively calm down, leaving her vulnerable to further behavioural explosions when in this state. She won't have an effective 'inside guide' that can lead her away from the intense emotions and explosive behaviour.

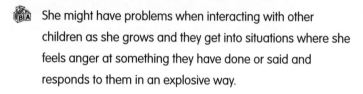 She might have problems when interacting with other children as she grows and they get into situations where she feels anger at something they have done or said and responds to them in an explosive way.

The consequences of interpersonal problems might lead her to have problems in relationships in general, as she would be unable to regulate or manage her intense emotions well and people might decide it's just too hard to be in a relationship with her.

To be honest, writing this now and thinking about these possible outcomes for my beloved little girl does my head in, especially if this type of outcome has been very much influenced by the way I taught her to react to situations and manage her intense emotions.

So, on to **the avenue to the right of the fork:** Put my arms around her and give her a cuddle — help her to calm down. Let her cry and say she is sorry. Let her tell me it was an accident. Tell her I know she is upset because she broke my watch. Tell her that I understand she didn't mean to. Thank her for saying sorry. Tell her that I am sorry for yelling at her too. Let her know that while I still feel sad that my watch is broken, the angriness is over now.

What this reaction would require of me: To put my daughter's need to be comforted ahead of my urge to continue ranting and raving. To keep my daughter in mind as opposed to just my feelings about what she did. To employ a strategy to calm myself down and dissolve my anger, or at least put it aside until I can work through it. To remember that I am a model for her at that moment. To make it a priority to teach her a way to manage anger and frustration by showing her how I do it. To remember I need to communicate in a way that she at her age understands — simply and concretely.

What this reaction would require of her: To allow me to comfort her. To not run off; to listen. To trust that I will not explode about it again.

The consequences: She can regain calmness more quickly, and from being calm she can hear what I say and get to a place where she can understand sooner rather than later. On a grander scale she will learn:

- Her relationship with me can weather storms as well as calm, peaceful waters.

- That when she makes mistakes she can have some power in being able to 'fix' them — staying there and saying sorry.

- To sit with uncomfortable experiences and work through them.

- To minimise the onset of feelings of shame and development of defensive mechanisms.

To see conflict as an opportunity to be worked through as opposed to being overwhelmed by it.

She can more effectively learn to process and discuss difficult moments with people.

The lessons our children receive on 'emotion' and 'emotional management' first come from us, their parents. As pressure loaded as this is, it's just the way it is. So it is an unavoidable part of parenting that we might on at least one occasion witness our children display their frustration, for example, in the same way we do. And often this is not one of our proud parenting moments — there is certainly no better feedback to bring home the message that we are models for our children!

We teach our children how comfortable they can be at having a range of feelings, with how much ease they can look at their feelings, whether they express them or not, how they express them and, eventually, how they exert control over them. We do all this by the way we speak about feelings to them (if we choose to bring theirs and other people's feelings into conversations and into play with them); how tolerant we are of feelings — both the easier ones and the more difficult ones — and how we display our own emotional expression and emotional management to them, either directly when interacting with them or indirectly through how we are around other people.

I personally think that it is this part of parenting that is trickiest because we are essentially people bringing up people. We have our own emotional histories and emotional 'training'; we have gone through our own period of being taught what to do with *our* emotions, and this influences how we express and manage emotion and how comfortable we are with feelings in general. And our *ways* of emotional management might not have been tested out in quite the same way that parenting tends to. Because of all this, the most unexpected things can come out of our mouth, things that before being authentically in the parenting role we would have *never* thought we would say!

How healthy our models were, how much conscious work we've done to bring about some change in our not so healthy components, and also how much conscious work we are prepared to continue doing, will all influence the lessons we give to our children on emotional management.

What is emotional regulation?

Emotional regulation is the ability to monitor and control the expression of emotion. It is a very important part of overall emotional development. A major reason it is important is because it helps us to make and maintain relationships. It is very difficult to be in a relationship with someone who can't regulate their emotions very well. An obvious example is a person who finds it difficult to regulate their anger. Think about being with someone who can't contain their anger or who can't calm down; who expresses their anger by yelling or by even more aggressive behaviour; who can't easily move forward to any type of rational stance but seems to get stuck in the anger and explosiveness of it all.

Hmm …

Now think about being in a relationship with someone who, when feeling angry, can identify that they are angry, express it in a non-harmful way, who can calm themselves down, can control any outbursts that their anger might push them towards and who, despite being angry, can manage their emotions in a way that allows them to keep moving forward in a productive manner.

It is much easier to be around people who are able to regulate their emotions.

Our babies grow into children, adolescents and then adults in a social world that revolves around relationships. So if they can be a person who is able to regulate their emotions effectively, it can certainly make life easier for them.

What we are aiming for

Through my work as a psychologist with adults, I have spoken to many people — mainly of the older generation — who had an upbringing that didn't allow for the easy expression of emotion. As a result, I have often thought of the opening verse of John Lennon's song 'Crippled Inside'. It describes how even though someone might be able to maintain a polished external appearance they're not able to hide being 'crippled inside'.

We can't hide being 'crippled inside' when it comes to our relationships. It's as if our relationships are the measure for how well developed our inside, emotional parts are. So when it comes to our children, brought up to exist in this 'relationship world', it will be of help to them if we can keep the amount they are 'crippled inside' to a minimum. Being continuously aware of their emotional development is a start.

When parenting, it is easy to focus on the parts of development that can be seen — sleeping, toileting, crawling, walking, activities, academics, IQ — things that can be easily measured and compared against norms and peers. But helping our kids to have a robust EQ (emotional intelligence) might not be consciously thought about. It can be easy to forget that healthy emotional development can underpin a child's ability to accomplish the seen things. For example, if a young child has a poor ability to manage emotions and hasn't internalised effective ways to calm themselves when feeling intense emotion, it might be all the more difficult to settle in at school. The behaviour that springs from their emotions might receive an unfair amount of focus and affect their ability to get on well with other kids, to listen to the teacher and to concentrate. In a traditional school setting, this might ultimately impact on the child's ability to learn and achieve at school. Our kids' strong emotions can exert a lot more power than they deserve if no attention is paid to nurturing and shaping them.

Perhaps because emotions are not easily seen, or perhaps not displayed by babies and toddlers in ways that are easily understood, or perhaps because there hasn't been a great deal of information available on the topic until relatively recently, the emotional world of babies and toddlers often isn't looked at much. But it's important to take some time to understand it.

I always think of a three-legged dog when it comes to emotional development in people. A bit weird, I know, but bear with me. For a dog to walk properly it ideally needs four legs. But it is not that uncommon to see here and there the occasional three-legged dog. These dogs haven't got the ideal walking set-up but they are still able to get about by learning to do without their fourth leg. When I see one of these dogs I'm torn between thinking, 'That's great; they're still able to get on with things', and,

'But it's so unfortunate because things could be so much easier for them — they're meant to have four legs.' Walking around with poorly developed emotional parts is a bit like being one of these dogs: we can get by and mostly we are unaffected, but when it comes to being in a relationship or interacting with someone on a deeper than superficial level, we sometimes realise the limitations of could-be-better emotional parts.

Helping our kids to thrive in what can be seen as well as in what cannot be so easily seen — their emotional skills — would be a good outcome for us to aim for as parents, as it's something we can do to make their lives a little bit easier. Or, to put it another way, it would be better if they weren't three-legged dogs ...

Just as we might have ideas about how we'd like to teach them to sleep, how we'd like to toilet train them and what activities we'd like them to be involved in, it is important to say to ourselves, 'And how I'd like them to function in relationships is ...' And because how they develop emotionally impacts on how they function in a relationship, we could continue by saying, 'And how I'd like them to be emotionally is ...'

When setting the goals for emotional development we are basically aiming for our children to be fairly emotionally intelligent throughout their lives — to have the ability to tune into their emotions and express them in ways that aren't going to wreck things for them. This will help them make and maintain relationships. As with all aspects of development, their set of genes as well as their natural personality (or temperament) will determine their potential as well as their limits, but their experiences and interactions can influence the shape their emotional 'parts' take.

Good emotional development might look like:

- The ability to identify their emotions accurately;

- The ability to experience the range of emotions (including the more 'difficult' ones);

- The ability to express (verbally and behaviourally) their emotions appropriately and adaptively (as opposed to maladaptively);

- The ability to perceive other people's emotions and adapt their own emotions accordingly;

- The ability to exert self-control over their emotions, particularly if their emotion at a particular time is going to put them in a potentially damaging situation (e.g. can't control anger in an argument with a friend or partner).

More specifically, successful emotional regulation might look like:

- Despite feeling a strong or positive emotion, they are able to curb or stop an inappropriate behaviour associated with the emotion;

- The ability to calm their nervous system down rather than continuing to ignite it;

- The ability to focus enough to meet a goal despite feeling strong emotions.

This picture of how we would like our children to be in terms of their emotional development is important to keep in mind. It's the long-term outcomes that can motivate us to put in the necessary effort. They can be what drag us back from the brink of our own emotional meltdowns! Keeping our eye on the prize (the prize being potentially emotionally well-rounded kids who grow into emotionally well-rounded adults) will hopefully remind us that what we are ultimately doing as parents is training our kids to be certain types of people who function in certain ways to get on in particular situations as grown-ups. And it all starts in babyhood and toddlerhood.

A way to start thinking about emotional regulation

Just as little ones need to be taught how to go to the toilet, they also need to be taught how to regulate or exert self-control over their emotions. As babies grow into toddlers they come across more varied emotions in varying intensities but don't yet have the brain capacity to express these emotions in ways that would be deemed acceptable to many of the people around them. This leaves them vulnerable to potential consequences. The ways in which young children display their natural, normal emotions can be met by a lot of different responses which are influenced by such things as our particular perspective on their little display, how we were taught to deal with emotion, our expectations of our children, our current stress levels and even things like the time of day, tiredness levels and how 'good' or 'bad' the day has been generally. So having a way to think about their emotional display and develop a perspective on it can be helpful, especially during the times when it is difficult to put on our own brakes to stop us from losing it.

So, to the toilet …

Toileting isn't a bad analogy to use when talking about learning how to manage emotions. Kids have to wee and poo — that's a fact. Kids have emotions — that's a fact too. Where to put it all is what they need to be taught. And who teaches them? We, their parents and carers, do.

When toddlers learn to go to the toilet, they basically learn to associate a full bladder or full bowel with going to the toilet to empty that fullness. When kids are first learning that the toilet is the appropriate place to go when needing to do number ones and number twos, there are usually a few accidents here and there — number twos in brand new undies or number ones on the carpeted floor of the newsagent. And when this happens, we somehow push past the frustration or embarrassment. We are fully aware that we are teaching them an important life skill and that it takes time, so we might wipe their tears away, give them a cuddle and reassure them that, 'It's okay, you're only learning.' We might reflect on how we can better help them next time; how we might be able to pick up on cues earlier so we can prompt them to go to the toilet; or teach them how to recognise for themselves the signs that they need to go.

But do we do this when they have their emotional spills? Is it as easy to remember when they are doing their *emotional* number ones and twos? Do we teach them that there are appropriate and inappropriate ways to empty their emotional 'fullness'? Do we comfort and soothe them and let them know that, 'It's okay, you're only learning'? Do we make it a priority to look out for their individual cues that might indicate they need to show emotion? And then do we think to prompt them to express it?

The answers probably vary depending on what else is happening at the time. When we are feeling calm and relaxed we might generally respond in this way. But when we are stressed, it is easy to get caught up in our own emotions and our own circumstances and not have our eyes open enough to be able to clearly see our kids' emotional needs. When we take a portrait photo with a good camera, the focus is on the face and the background becomes fuzzy. In the same way, when we are stressed, our issue is in focus and our kids' emotional needs are in the background and a bit out of focus.

This makes me think of a section in a book called *Parenting from the Inside Out* by Daniel J. Siegel and Mary Hartzell that makes a lot of sense to me. They talk about responding to our kids from the 'high road' or from the 'low road'; i.e. from a higher mode of brain processing or from a lower mode of processing. Ideally, we would want to be on the high road most of the time, as it is in this mode that we have our whole brain available to us and, most importantly, the parts that enable us to handle challenging parenting situations well: the ability to consider what is going on for our child, the ability to be self-aware, to be reflective, flexible and creative in responding to them. But sometimes we end up on the low road, and in this mode we aren't able to do all those things I just listed. It's as if we are cut off from those abilities. Instead, we are stuck in some type of intense emotion unhelpful to the situation, such as rage, and all our responses to our kids come from the perspective of this intense emotion instead of from a calm, more rational perspective. So we might yell or act in an impulsive, inconsiderate manner.

I find this high road/low road way of responding very useful when talking about emotional regulation because it provides a structure on which to hang our 'normalcy'. Sometimes we are able to respond to our kids' emotional spills calmly and most helpfully, but there are other times when we just don't. If our natural way of managing our own heightened emotions could be better, and we have to put in more effort to respond to our kids in a rational way during these times, then being stressed leaves us vulnerable to losing the ability to put in this conscious effort.

The authors of the high road/low road concept talk about how it is the unresolved issues that parenting can trigger that take us off the high road and send us hurtling down the low road. It is a very interesting parenting book to read as it puts the focus on the parent — it helps parents be aware of their own 'stuff' so to speak, and how this 'stuff' can come out in parenting. Obviously it goes into the high road/low road situation in greater depth and detail than I can do here, but I would like to borrow this concept and hold it up as a point of reference for ourselves when dealing with our children's emotions. The high road is something we can refer to and strive for when we are thrown into emotional spins by our kids' behaviour and their emotional number ones and twos. While I am aware that I might not perhaps be using their concept in the way the authors originally intended — and I apologise for that — to me it makes sense to use the idea of high-road responses and low-road responses as a way to be mindful of how our emotions influence the way we respond to our children.

Will I take the high road or the low road?

When trying to deal with a situation that is sending our emotional state into volcano mode, building in a simple question like: 'Was that a high-road response or am I on the low road?' might help us to be more aware of our own emotional responses to our kids at the time. As a parent, however, I know this is often easier said than done when actually in an emotional tangle with kids. So if we can somehow be mindful enough at those times to ask ourselves that question and it has the effect of turning us around a bit — fantastic. But we might very well miss the chance. As the authors of the concept outline, being on the low road means it is difficult to access the parts of our brain that would easily allow us to be aware and calm enough to ask ourselves such a question. It might therefore be easier to have a plan, namely to remain calm enough to remember we have a choice in how we respond. Our choice, of course, is 'Will I take the high road or the low road here?'

The Plan

Step One: Stay calm

Step Two: Remember we have a choice

Step Three: Decide to respond from the high-road position

Step Four: Actually try to do it

N.B. WE MAY HAVE TO REPEAT 'STEP ONE' SEVERAL TIMES!

Much of the effort involved in trying to respond as much as possible from the high road lies in trying to avoid going down the low road. When we are in a mind state that makes it easy to respond from the high road, then no problem: our goal has been achieved. It's when we are in not such a good state that we have to put in the effort.

It is important to work on intervening *before* getting on the low road if at all possible, or at least getting off it as quickly as we can. This requires us to increase our awareness about ourselves in general because what we need to do to intervene early is to notice when we are getting worked up, notice if we are at that stage emotionally where it is a real possibility that we will go down the low road, and intervene *then*.

In the real-life example at the start of this chapter, the road to the left is an example of a low-road response and the road to the right is more of a high-road response. When in the throes of raw emotion, it is very difficult to switch to the other road. It is often necessary to put ourselves in 'time out' so that we are able to achieve Step One of our plan: calm down. After all, using the time-out strategy is common when little ones are responding from *their* low road — when they are yelling, throwing, hitting or generally behaving in a way that is not helpful to all. If our little

people could talk they might send us to the time-out spot when we are coming at them from *our* low road!

In quieter moments it can be productive for us to look at ourselves and work towards developing an insight into our less than 'parent of the year' moments. These moments can often end in a huge dump of guilt and even feelings of shame. It is easy to get bogged down by these feelings, but this doesn't help anyone. So perhaps next time one of those 'moments' comes along, acknowledge the guilt and shame, but instead of focusing on the heaviness of those feelings, focus on being proactive. This is where we move into Step Two of our plan: remembering we have a choice in how we respond.

It can be useful to spend some time reflecting on the moment and turning it into a data-collecting exercise. We could try to identify the point at which we could have intervened to take us onto the high road instead of full speed down the low road. We could also reflect on the point at which it was too late — when there was no going back — so we know for next time. We can reflect on what it was that made us react in the first place: is it the same type of behaviour or emotional display from our little ones that led to our moment? Is there a pattern? Reflect on what makes us particularly vulnerable: is there something about us that is always present when a moment arrives? Are we excessively tired or stressed perhaps or, dare I say it, might it be that time of the month? Reflect on how we could best identify that feeling earlier next time. How did we experience the huge surge of emotion that led to the moment? Where did it seem to sit in our body? Did it feel like our head was exploding or perhaps our chest or stomach or even our whole body?

This type of information is important if we want to bring

about some sort of change in the way we respond; in other words, if we want to use Step Three in the plan and respond from the high road as much as possible.

By looking at ourselves in this way we are developing insight and increasing our awareness. After all, we can't change what we aren't really aware of. By gathering this type of information we open up the possibility for us to use the plan next time and see what happens.

So let's move onto Step Four: actually trying to respond from the high-road position. It may help to take a bit of an experimental approach. Instead of being determined to 'get it right', we can perhaps simply see if we can be more mindful of our feelings, see if we can stay calm, see if we can remember we have a choice and, ultimately, see what happens if we choose to adopt a response different to the usual one. Does it divert our path from the low road and towards the high road? We can fine-tune our response further with each attempt.

Developing emotional regulation

The ideal is to respond to our children as much as possible from the high road and also to teach our children to respond as much as possible from the high road themselves — to make them as emotionally intelligent as possible. Of course, the high road is 'under construction' during their baby and childhood years. This is because emotional regulation is a higher-level process that sits in a part of the brain that is not developed at birth — but remember that we contribute to the construction process.

As was outlined in Chapter One, various parts of a baby's brain develop as a result of interaction with others. And the quality and frequency of the interaction influence the way in which the areas of the brain develop. When it comes to emotional regulation, the way babies are interacted with influences how the parts that are assigned to emotional monitoring, expression and control operate. So if we want our children to respond from the high road as they

grow older, they will need the brain parts to be organised in a way that supports them being able to do so. The best chance of this happening relies upon us trying to interact with them from the high road as consistently as possible right from babyhood. Regulating our behaviour around our babies falls under the heading of quality interaction.

To interact with our babies in a way that provides them with quality emotional regulation requires us to be emotionally in tune with them, to be in tune with what they might be feeling and need. Just as we tune in to music on the radio, we can tune in to how our babies might be feeling. Sometimes it can take a while to hear the music on the radio clearly, and often we go through a patch of scratchy static before the music comes through crystal clear. It's much the same when we try to tune in to how our babies are feeling: it can take a while to get it right, for their feelings to be crystal clear.

From our babies' point of view, we want them to feel understood, to feel that someone 'gets' them, that they have been 'heard'. Being in tune with them and their emotions can give them this sense. This shouldn't come as a surprise as we respond the same way. When someone is in tune with *our* feelings when we need them to be, we feel validated, which in turn brings a feeling of relief because we don't have to keep trying to get someone to listen and really understand. If that person continues to tune in fairly consistently to us we develop a conviction that they just 'get us' and we can begin to relax and trust that this is the person who understands us most. We can be completely honest and free in our expression because we know they will understand, regardless of whether the emotion we are expressing falls into the 'positive emotion' basket or the 'negative emotion' basket.

How do we tune in?

One of the most basic but effective skills when counselling someone is 'reflective listening'. This is essentially reflecting back to the person you are counselling what they have said to you in your own words. But you don't just reflect their words back to them; you also reflect their emotions. You communicate back to them what they are trying to convey *overall*. For example:

*Person (**with worried expression**): Since being at uni I haven't been able to keep on top of the heap of other things in my life. It's all over the place.*

Reflective listener: You have to juggle a lot of things in your life now and you are worried you are losing control of them.

Reflective listening requires us to tune into a person as much as possible. It's understanding where they are coming from, hearing the feelings they are experiencing not just their words, and communicating this back to them in a way that makes them feel you 'get it'. To be able to do this well requires the ability to be still, in body and mind, so that you can really listen and observe the person as they express what they are saying.

This is essentially what we do to tune in to our babies and their emotional needs. By being still, staying calm and observing, we have a better chance of really hearing what they are trying to communicate. It is very useful to develop the skill to be still and observe. Regardless of how naturally attuned we are as parents, being still and observing our children at every age and stage (as opposed to jumping straight into action) will probably prove to be a golden tool on our parenting tool belt.

Of course, when it comes to babies it's a little tricky to understand what they are 'saying' when their only means of communication are things like their cry and other sounds; their facial expressions; skin tone; and their little bodies. So at this stage of their lives, our ability to be still and observe is particularly useful. Not only do we observe them for what they might be trying to tell us but also for the context in which they are expressing the emotion and need. Do they look content or uncomfortable? Do they look tired? How long has it been since they've been fed? Is there a lot of stimulation around them? How would we feel in this situation? We look for clues and come up with hypotheses as to what they might be 'saying'. And we observe their display of emotion while keeping in mind that one of the reasons they are showing emotion is so that they can engage with us (when it comes to the positive range of emotions) or get help from us to feel better (when it comes to the more difficult-to-handle emotions). They haven't the ability to tell us with words that they have needs. Very young babies can't say, 'I am extremely upset,' nor can they do anything at all about soothing themselves; they are completely reliant on us to do it for them. They are extremely vulnerable and at the mercy of how we treat and interact with them.

We are literally their regulators, because they don't have the brain capability yet to regulate themselves. So it's as if *we* are the regulating part of their brain until it develops and they can take on that function themselves. When we are sensitive to their needs, emotionally tuned into them and consistent in our responses, they learn that their upset feelings pass by being soothed. Over time they become able to tolerate small amounts of distress because they know that help is not far away and that the help can be relied upon to deliver.

As they get older and become more mobile, they are able to reach for things that bring them comfort, like their thumb, blankies, dummies and cuddlies. They can also turn away when they feel overwhelmed, which doesn't take much because their little nervous systems can easily become overloaded. They use these newfound skills to regulate themselves as they grow older. When they are old enough to understand the concept of time out, letting them know that they can 'come out when they have calmed down and are ready to get on with things' teaches them they have control over their feelings. If we do the same thing when we are 'high with emotion', the lesson is reinforced. So their ability to self-regulate emotion is developed through a combination of us continuing to assist them by being their 'regulators', them using their own self-regulatory skills as they develop, and our modelling of appropriate behaviour.

Being still and observing allows us to also strike that balance between not noticing an emotional need and being really intrusive.

| **Not noticing** | **BALANCE** | **Intrusive** |

It is easy to misinterpret babies' cues and in our anxiety to 'get it right' we might actually be adding to their upset feelings sometimes due to too much action and not enough observation. An example of this can occur when children develop the ability to physically turn away as they get older and gain more control of their body. What they are trying to do by turning away when they are distressed is turn off the overwhelmed feeling. They can't speak and say, 'Stop it please, I don't like it!' as we teach our toddlers to do. They can only use what skills they are developmentally capable of. But if we aren't mindful that they might be turning away because they feel overwhelmed, we can become intrusive and follow them, pursuing them even after they've turned away from us.

It's helpful to keep in mind questions like: 'Could it be possible she is turning away because she is overwhelmed by something?', 'Am I misinterpreting her turning away from me as her not wanting me?', 'Am I pursuing a more favourable response from her?', 'Do I need to just wait and watch her a bit more to work out what might be happening?'

So while we might have to take a trial and error approach and experiment with getting it right, simply by being *mindful* that our babies are expressing emotion, being *mindful* that when they turn away from us they might be trying to switch off a feeling that is overwhelming them, being responsive to their expression of emotion, *consistent* in how we react to it and *giving them space* to use their own ways of regulating their behaviour as they grow older, we will be helping them because our focus is in the right direction: towards them.

We might feel helpless during times of trying to get it right, but our efforts are not wasted. From where our babies are lying, they notice that we are trying to tune into them and that they are getting something good from being at the receiving end of this attentive, sensitive interaction. We might perceive our efforts as fumbling and all wrong, but to them they just see their mum's/dad's/carer's eyes looking at them, feel the warmth of being picked up and cuddled, hear soothing words, and smell the familiar, comfortable smells of the person they love most in the world. Even if we take some time to work things out, we're still providing some kind of balance to their upset feelings.

What are we doing for them?

Our babies are forming, through our attentive, albeit sometimes confused efforts to soothe them, an inside model of how emotions work. I can imagine a baby being interviewed about what they've picked up from their parents' responses to their emotional expression. If they could articulate what they are

SO, WHAT HAVE YOU LEARNED ABOUT EMOTIONS FROM YOUR PARENTS?

actually internalising through our inter-actions with them as they grow, it might go something like:

'Well, I've learned lots of things that I will definitely remember as I grow up. When I'm upset they pick me up and comfort me. From that I've learned that that's what you do with upset feelings — comfort and soothe somehow. My body has become used to this.

When I'm happy they join in and it's fun.

When I'm feeling some sort of feeling enough to express it, they notice it — that must mean that feelings are important. And whether the emotion I express is a 'good' one or a 'difficult' one they still respond to it in a decent way. That must mean that all feelings are okay, and I'm still accepted and loved when I'm carrying on a bit.

As I've grown into my basic abilities to self-regulate my feelings, they seem mindful of this and give me the space to use them. This makes me feel a bit more confident that I can actually calm myself down. I think I'm achieving real growth here.

So I'm starting to get it now. It's okay to feel all kinds of different feelings, it's okay to express them — I'll be loved *regardless. When I'm happy they join in and that feels even better, and I'm starting to know the kind of feelings that need some sort of soothing and calming down. By them calming me down when I've needed them to all this time, I can now put up with feeling upset for a bit longer because I know and trust that they will help me out. I've also started to develop my own ways to help myself calm down, which they've given me the space to use. I feel like I've got a good 'inside guide' plus a small repertoire of self-regulating skills of my own. Overall, I feel good about how my emotional model is starting to take shape.'*

When they turn verbal

As our babies start to use words it's as if another world opens up for them. Finally they have a way to communicate efficiently with those big people! By the time they can speak, their brain has developed more of an ability to think in terms of past and future instead of just in the moment, so the world is a much bigger and more detailed place. And finally we parents also have a common means of communicating! There's a certain thrill attached to listening to little mouths trying to form the words of our language. Sometimes realisation strikes that they really are people when they are not only walking but speaking like us too (or trying to). I have delighted in the mispronunciation of words that have come out of my kids' mouths. It really brings home their innocence and just how 'junior' they are as humans. On the one hand it illustrates how far they've come in their development from brand new little babies, but on the other hand it emphasises that they continue to need a huge amount of guidance to function in the world they are being brought up to exist in.

As adults, we fully understand how easy it makes things to have a handle on language. We try to instil the use of words in our little ones as a way to efficiently communicate needs — 'Use your words!' But, like everything else, they need to be taught how to do this.

The sort of words they use depends on the sort of words they hear a lot. And the context they use them in comes from the context they hear them used in most. This becomes very evident when we first hear our little one, in appropriate context, drop a swear word that may or may not be used regularly around the home ...

In the same way that they learn to use a swear word through hearing it used regularly by someone (just *who* we might never know!), they will also learn to use words to describe how they

are feeling if they hear words being used that way on a regular basis. It's never too early to start using words to describe how they are feeling. As young babies, they don't understand the words in the same way we do, but they are definitely capable of learning. How else are they able to say their first word when they eventually do? By hearing words repeatedly associated with the thing it corresponds to, they learn what a word means. So by saying something like, 'You're tired' in a calm, soothing voice while comforting a tired baby, the baby will gradually learn to associate the word 'tired' with the state of tiredness.

I'm not saying that we should expect our toddlers' first words to be, 'I'm feeling frustrated' or 'I'm ecstatically happy at the moment'. But as babies, they can start to grow accustomed to hearing certain words used when they experience the corresponding feelings. And it is as much about training ourselves as it is about training them. If we start developing this emotional language early with them, we will be very au fait with it by the time they start to use the words themselves.

Why the need for an emotional language?

When our children start to use words, their ability to communicate their needs steps up to a new level. Being able to communicate their emotional needs will stand them in good stead as they come across different feelings and their world grows more complex. If they grow up with it being normal to talk about their 'inside' world — to bring it from inside to 'outside' — they might find it easier to sort out things in a timely manner and move forward. This will be helpful as they get into spats with playmates, navigate their way through their school years and get involved in intimate relationships. It will prove invaluable to have a 'language' to communicate to us, and others like teachers and counsellors, what is behind their behaviour at times.

This is because behaviours can be good smoke screens; it isn't always obvious what feelings are behind children's behaviour. The way children show their feelings is 'flavoured' by their personality, just as it is with us. Typically kids are either more 'outward' in their behaviour expression or 'inward'. The smoke screen that the outward expression provides is behaviour that can be easily seen. This is the sort of behaviour that they can get into trouble for, and therefore, the focus can easily be limited to the behaviour itself; it is easy to forget that there is a feeling behind the behaviour. Inward behaviours are more subtle and fit with being more socially acceptable, if you like. These behaviours don't often lead to children getting into trouble but they can lead to children being easily overlooked — and therefore the feeling behind the 'inward' behaviour is left unexplored.

Any way feelings manifest themselves can be easily misinterpreted if there isn't a good combination of invested interest, quiet observation, detective skills and asking the question, 'Could there be a feeling behind this particular display?' Trying to work out what is going on for a child when they are struggling emotionally can be a bit like a detective show in which all the clues are collected and put together like pieces of a puzzle until the mystery is solved. If children had well-developed abilities and a comfortable forum in which to say, 'I'm feeling sad because ...' it might cut down the length of the show from that of a marathon movie to a TV episode!

Children will struggle emotionally to varying degrees — it's virtually a fact of life. As heartbreaking as the thought of our little ones struggling at any age is, it is in our (and their) best interests to accept it rather than resist it. They need us to have our eyes open, not closed, to their emotional struggles because, as in everything else to do with growing up, children need to be taught what to do with their feelings. They need help and guidance right from the start. Building in this help and guidance as part of their foundations sets the pattern for what *they* will do and how *they* will operate as people around the issue of feelings and emotions.

It's helpful for us as well because as they get older we will want to know what is going on inside them and how certain life events impact on them. It would be unreasonable to expect them to answer the common question of, 'What's wrong?' if they haven't been taught to look at themselves in a way that would enable them to get a good sense of 'what is wrong'. And as they experience a variety of interactions, some questions just pop out of our mouths, such as: 'How did you feel when that happened?' Answering such questions would be a hard task without some lessons in the language of emotions. The basic lessons are:

- To name feelings;

- To have the words to describe how they are feeling in relation to events and situations;

- To know that some feelings need 'repairing' or 'fixing' — their own as well as other people's;

To intervene in the 'troublesome' feelings as early as possible;

 To feel genuinely comfortable to talk about their feelings.

How do we teach them?

There are numerous educational games that can help children to learn about feelings, but we can also do some teaching of our own. We teach them by the way *we* talk about feelings. Using the swear-word acquisition technique above, we can build emotional words into our general day-to-day conversations with them right from babyhood through to adolescence. This comes more easily to some of us than others, depending on our own individual upbringing around emotions. At some point a conscious decision might need to be made to include 'feeling speak' into conversations, but it's important to strike a nice balance and not overdo it — we don't want our kids to start rolling their eyes at the very mention of the word 'feelings'!

So by tuning in and using our observation skills, we can sensitively choose times to help them learn the basic lessons of emotional language.

Lesson 1: Name feelings

We 'name feelings' for them. For example, 'You're feeling frustrated', 'You're feeling sad', 'You're excited aren't you!' When we accurately name their feelings, they learn the difference between them; it allows them to differentiate between the feeling states they experience. As mentioned above, naming feelings can start from a very young, pre-speaking age. If we do this consistently, over time our kids will internally sort their feelings into categories, making them easier to organise and refer to when they've developed enough to describe how they feel. It's kind of like having a filing cabinet labelled 'Feelings'. By naming their feelings from early on, their filing cabinet has a better chance of being well organised as opposed to messy and chaotic.

Lesson 2: Describe their feelings in relation to things

By linking the feeling to an action — 'You're feeling frustrated because you can't have that toy', 'You're feeling sad because she said she wasn't your friend', 'You're excited because it is your birthday' — we help our kids to learn a bit about why they are having the feeling. It helps them to understand it a little more and realise that feelings are usually localised to a certain event or situation rather than being huge, general, overwhelming waves. This can have the effect of simplifying things for them. Part of the lesson learned is that experiencing a certain (upset) feeling doesn't have to equal disaster. It is just a feeling brought about by something; having feelings is a normal part of life. Being able to pinpoint why they are having a certain feeling adds more information to the situation and this will help efforts to move on from a troublesome feeling (with some help and guidance).

And if you think about any assertiveness training you might have done, it usually revolves around learning the skills to be able to say, 'I'm feeling _____ because _____.' That is, you learn to link a feeling with something and communicate the link. As our kids begin to use sentences fairly easily, we can encourage them to link in this way to aid the way they communicate. It can help to resolve situations a lot more efficiently. Building in guided encouragement such as, 'You are feeling sad because ...?' helps them to make the links.

Lesson 3: Some feelings need fixing — theirs and others'

The idea of 'repairing' or 'fixing' feelings is an important part of having feelings. Knowing what they can do to help themselves calm down or feel comforted is an example of fixing their own feelings. Saying 'sorry' is an example of trying to fix other people's feelings.

In combination with providing ongoing consistent responses to their emotional display, we can guide them with words to identify feelings that could be 'fixed' and equip them with ways in which to do it. For example, 'You are very angry and it's making you hit the wall. You need to calm down. How about you go to your room for a while/cuddle your teddy/lie down/play outside/take some deep breaths?' When reading stories or watching TV, the feelings of the characters can be focused on and possible solutions to fix feelings can be explored: 'What do you think the dog is feeling? What do you think he could do to feel better? Maybe he could cuddle his blanket.'

When it comes to fixing other people's feelings, it is a necessary first step to instil in them the notion that their actions and words can bring about feelings in other people. For example, 'I feel sad because you hit me,' and 'You hurt my feelings when you said that' and 'I know you are frustrated, but it is not okay to hit me. It hurts.' This will help them to develop the idea that other people have feelings too; it will help them towards developing empathy and being able to 'tune in' to feelings, which are important skills to have on board when interacting with other people. While developmentally young kids are at the 'centre of the universe' (egocentric) stage, gently shaping their empathy skills by sensitively teaching them that what they say and do can cause others to feel a certain way can aid their overall social skills.

Knowing that they can cause other people to have feelings is the first step. Knowing how to fix them when needed is the next. Using questions like: 'How can you fix my feelings?' combined with suggested ways like: 'You can say you are sorry' and 'You can give me a cuddle' helps to expand their repertoire of emotional skills. They learn they can bring about change to other people's feelings by taking some simple steps. Tapping into and reinforcing their strengths can also be effective: 'You're a kind person. How can you use your kindness to fix my feelings?'

The way we model behaviour is another way children learn to fix feelings. Apologising to them or to another person for having 'gone off the deep end' unnecessarily is one way to do this. You can simply take a deep breath and say something like: 'I got very angry a little while ago and said _____ I shouldn't have said that and I am very sorry.' Remembering to do this can be difficult sometimes but it is an important part of overall anger management and is considered healthy 'argument etiquette'. Our kids are going to get angry and they are going to argue, so we may as well try to teach them good etiquette.

It's important to remember that our kids need to be taught this stuff; they don't just know how to do it. It is a way of using language and behaviour that we might take for granted or might never have learned. It is easy to forget that kids literally need to be told and shown how to handle their feelings. Similarly, they also need to be taught how to intervene in those feelings that can get out of hand and lead them into trouble.

Lesson 4: Intervene in the 'troublesome' feelings as early as possible

When something requires intervention, the adage to live by is 'the earlier the better'. When it comes to intervening in a heightened emotion this couldn't be more appropriate. When feelings are felt strongly, they can lead to behaviours that are equally strong. Knowing when to intervene is a very important skill: a lot of 'angry' adults have trouble with this and have to attend anger-management classes or counselling sessions to learn the necessary skills.

To try to avoid this outcome for our little ones, we can incorporate 'intervention techniques' into their emotional lessons from the beginning. We do it for them when they are very young by being responsive to their expression of emotion: we pick them up and comfort them with warm pats and soothing words. This is when we are literally their regulators. Our role as the regulator continues as they become verbal, just in a more complex form. Our efforts are assisted by their ability to understand and speak a bit more, but we essentially still need to let them know when they are getting worked up, help them to notice it within themselves and guide them to do something about it sooner rather than later. For example, 'I can see you are getting angry because you are starting to yell and hit. It's okay to feel angry but it's not okay to hurt other people. How about you calm down by going outside for a while?' As they get older we can still prompt them, but hand the reins over to them a bit more: 'It seems like your anger is getting a bit on top of you. How about you do something to calm down?'

This is not to say we 'cut off' their feelings. It is important for them to feel the range of emotions — if they are angry they are angry — but it's when those emotions reach a level that will potentially lead them down a path that could make matters worse for them that we can help them out.

Lesson 5: Feel genuinely comfortable to talk about their feelings

Speaking to our kids in these ways — acknowledging feelings in them and others, naming feelings, and including them as part of normal conversation right from the beginning — will 'set the scene' for how comfortable or uncomfortable talking about feelings is in particular families. But it also depends on how we respond to their display of emotion throughout their life as they grow older — and specifically, on the messages we send to them about emotions through our actions and words. Is it acceptable to have feelings and to express them, or not? Are there conditions? Is their information safe with us or will they hear it being told to other parents in the school ground? When they ask to speak to us do we appear to them as relaxed and open or frustrated with no time to spare? Do we let them know we will make time if it's not convenient now?

It also depends on how we react to their attempts to talk about their feelings when they are old enough. Are we mindful that we are trying to encourage this behaviour and make it a priority to make time for them or do we put it off and then not follow up? Do we show warm affection towards them and praise them for talking about their feelings regardless of what they are, or do we get angry at them for what they say? Are we good listeners and let them explain things using their words in their own time or do we interrupt them with 'solutions' to hurry up the conversation or out of sheer anxiety at hearing that they are struggling?

A bit more about school-age children

I want to make special mention here of children a bit older then the main focus of this book because when it comes to emotional development it is about playing the 'long game' not the 'short game'. By this I mean we are ultimately preparing our kids to deal with life. We want them to have the skills they need to get by the best way they can when life treats them well and also not so well. School is the time when they start to get more of a taste of what life can hold in store.

When our kids go to school they can experience some difficult times with emotions. So can we. It's easy to fall into that 'I need to fix it' mode. In a sense we have to be forgiven for this because that is exactly what we need to do for them when they are babies and toddlers. Plus it's a bit anxiety-provoking to know that our 'babies' (as they will always be to us, no matter how old they are) are feeling bad in some way. But as they get older, and especially as they reach the age when they head off to school, they are far more able to deal with things. Now it's our role to help them become more independent. It is easy to forget this though, and therefore easy to forget to pace ourselves in line with their development. Faced with still-chubby little faces and little bodies in too-big uniforms, it is easy to forget that our job as parents is to bring up people who eventually don't need to depend on their parents, who can survive in this world independently.

I am not saying that we stop helping and guiding. Our children most definitely still need us to help and guide them because they enter a whole new world of social interactions when they get to school. They are trying to navigate their way through relationships with other children and teachers with skills that are only in their infancy. But the help is in a different form from when they were younger. When they are younger our guidance is more directive; it's as if we walk behind them telling them where to go — 'Turn left now', 'Turn right now', 'Go straight ahead'. By putting in the effort when they are younger, we help them to internalise a lot of our 'teachings' so that as they grow older they kind of carry us with them as an 'inside guide'. But they still won't have come across some of the things they will encounter at school — their 'inside guide' can take them only so far; they will still need help to work some things through. Their 'inside guide' will need ongoing fine-tuning as they progress through their development. And this is where our ongoing presence comes in. Not as a directive 'in their face' presence, but as more of a 'close but more at a distance than before' presence. We will grow closer when they need us, and then they will let us go a bit — and they are meant to do that. They still need us to be there for them, as tuned-in and as consistently responsive as we have always been, but they also need a bit of room to move. They need to be able to test out what they have learned. Sometimes this will work out fine and other times it won't, and this is where we step in again. But we can only know that we need to step in if we are 'switched on' and using those simple techniques of being still, observant and mindful that we might be needed. These skills never go out of style and never decrease in effectiveness.

Chapter Five

SELF-AWARENESS AND OUR PARENTING VALUES

SOMETIMES WE NEED TO OBSERVE OURSELVES A LITTLE MORE CLOSELY

In the last chapter I spoke about the value in being still and observing our kids so we have a better chance at seeing their needs. In this chapter I want to talk about the value in being still and observing *ourselves*. There can be some good benefits to having the skill to observe ourselves — the woman in the cartoon above would certainly be able to appreciate them! To borrow a term from Acceptance and Commitment Therapy (ACT), developing and nurturing the 'observing self' in us can give us a better chance of being the type of parent we would really like to be. Our observing self is a perspective or a viewpoint; it's like we stand back from, or levitate above, ourselves (figuratively speaking) and notice

what we are thinking, how we are behaving, what we are saying, how we are interacting with our children and other people around us.

By being in our observing-self mode, we have the luxury of being in a space in which our thoughts and feelings don't control our actions, because we are not *in* our thoughts and feelings, we are *observing* them. By not being caught up in and carried away by our troublesome thoughts and feelings, it is easier to make the choices we'd like to more often. It's like when we suddenly become aware that we are putting chocolate after chocolate into our mouth while watching a movie: when we are mindlessly doing it, we are *in* the behaviour; when we become aware that we are doing it, we are *observing* the behaviour. We can keep doing it if we choose, but we don't have a choice if we are not aware.

We exercise our observing self by regularly observing, noticing and bringing things into our awareness. So here is an exercise to do some time to help you understand the concept of observing self. Get your little one and give them a cuddle. Use all your senses and really savour the experience. Be aware of everything about them: their hair, their skin, their smell, their breathing. *Notice* that you are giving them a cuddle. *Notice* what you feel like inside, what feelings you are experiencing, what thoughts you are having. And, if it's not too bizarre for you, even notice that you are noticing all this.

When we are doing this we are in our observing-self mode. This is the position we can adopt to view ourselves and our interactions with our babies and toddlers. Our observing self, through noticing our experience, helps us to be in the present moment as it is all happening. From being in the present moment, we can notice the thoughts, behaviours, words and general ways of interacting that are both consistent and inconsistent with our parenting values and how we really want to be as a mother/father/carer.

Using our observing self to keep sight of our parenting values

What are our values as a parent? What sort of parent do we really want to be? What matters to us as parents? What actions do we need to take on an ongoing basis to be this sort of parent? How do we want to interact with our children right from babyhood? What behaviours would indicate that we are being the parent we want to be throughout their lives? What would we like our kids to say about our relationship with them when they are adults and giving a speech at the 'Parenting of the Year' Award Ceremony after presenting us with our award? These are important questions to ask because the answers will reveal our parenting values.

To borrow once again from ACT, and specifically Steven Hayes, the founder of ACT, our values are like a compass. We use them to choose the direction in which we want to move and to keep us on track when we're travelling the parenting journey. We can use our values as a guide to the choices we make as parents. I like what Russ Harris, another ACT leader, says about how we can use our values in his book *ACT Made Simple*:

> *When you go on a journey, you don't want to clutch the compass tightly every step of the way — you want to carry it in your backpack, knowing that anytime you need it to steer a course or find your way, you can instantly pull it out and use it.*

I like this because it makes me feel reassured. To have an easy-to-access guide about the way we want to be as a parent and to guide the *way* we parent can be reassuring. It gives us a sense of what we are doing. And it comes from deep down inside us, not from any book; it's always with us. We look to our values to guide our actions. Basically, every now and then we ask, 'Would this behaviour/action be in accordance with my values as a parent or not?'

But to be able to ask this question in the first place and to be able to use our values as guides, we need to be in a position in which we can 'see' we have choices. And this brings me back to the observing self. If we are *in* our thoughts, feelings and behaviours, it is very difficult to see beyond them or outside them. It is not until we turn to our observing self that we 'see'

My Parenting Values
How I want to be as a parent

— I want to use my
'observing self' as
much as possible

whether we are behaving in a way that might be taking us away from our core values or towards them.

It is our observing self that keeps sight of our values and notices when we are at that fork in the road. It notices which thoughts are for the left and which are for the right. But it is up to us to *choose* which path to take. We don't have to *choose* the one that takes us closer to our values; if we do it's only because our values mean a lot to us.

So what means a lot to us as a parent? If we were to put together a list of how we want to *be* as a parent, what would be on it? This is a personal thing; if you haven't already worked out your values as a parent, perhaps have a go. Given the themes in this book, I suggest that tapping into our observing self as often as possible throughout our parenting be in the Top 10 inclusions.

Checking in with our observing self on a regular basis helps us to know whether or not we need to pull our compass out of our backpack for a quick bit of guidance. It can let us know if we are still on track or if we have stumbled and are lying lost in a ditch! Parenting can throw out days full of exhausting challenges at times, so it's good to be able to take stock of where we're at like this.

Using our observing self to be aware of our kids' perspective

Our observing self can also let us know if we are caught up in our own stuff too much — our own thoughts, feelings and behaviours. When we are caught up in *ours* we are less aware of *theirs*. I would like to offer that it is important we attempt to be aware of our children's minds, their perception of things, the motivation and feelings behind their behaviour, because by doing this we are attempting to really understand them. Our babies and kids will only benefit from this: having a sense of being understood gives them that relaxed, comfortable, 'aaah these people really get me and my needs' feeling. It helps them to develop trust and confidence, the freedom to express themselves, and a general sense of security around the people bringing them up.

We are in our big world with fully developed brains, adult abilities, experiences and ways of operating. Then we have our kids, who are in their little world in which everything is new and which they approach with fresh eyes and developing-as-they-go brains. We are in different worlds marked by, among others things, different lengths of time inhabiting them and developing in complexity. Our ability to understand our world can vary and is still an ongoing process (for me anyway). But while we might still be trying to work out some things, we generally have an idea of how to go about life: what we feel comfortable doing and what we don't; how we feel about certain things; the way we tend to think and behave in various situations and around certain people. Over time we've probably also developed ideas about some parts of 'our world'.

But our kids' ability to understand *their* world is an even more ongoing process — they are literally learning and downloading vital life information every day. They are in the very process of working out what they are comfortable and uncomfortable with, how they feel about things, and how to behave in various situations and around certain people. They constantly need our help with all this, and we can do a better job if we try as much as possible to see, hear and sense where they are coming from when they say or do things in certain ways. Part of this is remembering that their world is very different from ours and that they have very different perceptions and interpretations of what's going on around them than we do; their 'reality' is different from ours.

A common mistake a lot of us make is to be 'too adult' in our thinking when it comes to interpreting the 'world' of a child. By this I mean we make assumptions about what is happening for a child based on how we would think, feel, see it, etc., from our big, grown-up, fully developed, adult point of view. Sometimes it is very useful to ask ourselves, 'Well, how would I feel in this situation?' as a guide to help us understand our little ones, but at other times it can fuzz up our interpretation of things. It's not uncommon to hear adults say, 'Oh, he doesn't like me!' about a baby who cries when they look at him or a toddler who hides behind his mum with an unsmiling face instead of saying goodbye. But think about it from the baby's and toddler's points of view. There could be a multitude of reasons behind their responses. They could be tired, hungry, have been out for a while and their little nervous systems have had enough, hot, cold, uncomfortable, caught up in a really good game, still feeling sad or grumpy about something that happened earlier; the adult could have interrupted them abruptly or scared them by the way he spoke to them, or could have features that might look scary to a young child — yellow teeth, facial hair, a loud voice, be very tall. He might have bad breath.

Whatever the reason, the bottom line is that babies and toddlers don't have the cognitive ability to articulate to themselves 'I don't like that person', and then behave accordingly: 'So I will ignore them.' When we interpret young children's behaviour from *our* world instead of *theirs*, we forget this and make assumptions about that child. When we do this we give them adult qualities, but they simply haven't been around long enough to develop into these yet.

Children have a world of seeing, perceiving, feeling, thinking and interpreting that is unique to each individual child and is separate from ours as adults. Remembering that they have a different position in life — literally — and from this position see the same things we do but from a much more simplistic and logical-to-them-but-perhaps-not-to-us angle, will help us to extend our thinking beyond how *we* would react, perceive, think and feel in various situations. It might help us to say to ourselves, 'I wonder how they are seeing this from *their* eyes/thinking about this with *their* brains/feeling this in *their* bodies?' And to perhaps respect that they simply have a different perspective. After all, at some level of logic, their perspective is true for *them*.

As grown-ups, we have the ability to see things from our perspective *and* from our kids' perspective if we remember to and *choose* to. Our young children only have the ability to see things from *theirs* — it's important we remember this. They can only see, experience, feel and think about things from their little, innocent, still-developing perspective. In the above cartoon, it is the mum who has the ability to think to turn the bowl over to investigate why her son is so adamant the bowl is spotty. She has the ability to problem solve at more complex levels. Her young son doesn't have the same ability yet.

When trying to see things from our kids' perspective, it's not so much about getting it right every single time, but rather about valuing the attempt. If we genuinely value it as a worthwhile and important part of interacting with our kids, then we will more than likely try our best at it.

Our efforts to see things from their perspective will be tested most by their more 'negative' behaviours. When they are chucking a tantrum, we see their behaviour (as does everyone else if it is happening in the supermarket ...), and it is easy to get caught up in it — perhaps trying to stop it out of embarrassment or annoyance. But if our eyes are only on their behaviour we will not be able to see that they are actually carrying on for a reason. It might not be obvious or logical to us, but it is a reason nonetheless — a reason that *to them* is real. Just trying to keep this in mind is the key. If we perceive our young child carrying on as 'naughty' or 'manipulative', it will affect the way we interact with them. Our reaction is likely to be different than if we perceive them as 'learning to deal with something' or as 'upset by something'. This is when the saying 'If you go out looking for one thing that's all you'll ever find' is very relevant. If we always focus on their 'carry-on' behaviour and see it as 'naughty', for example, that's all we'll ever see. But if we approach their carry-on with a wider perspective — a perspective that includes their take on things, how they might be experiencing the situation — and look for the possible reasons behind it, then we might find more than our limited perspective allows.

I am referring here to the psychological process of 'mentalisation'. This is the ability to be aware of our and other people's feelings and to understand our and other people's behaviour in terms of underlying things such as individual needs, desires, feelings, beliefs, goals and reasons. I was introduced to this term by reading the work of Dr Arietta Slade on Parental Reflective Functioning, which incorporates mentalisation and broadly means the capacity to keep our children — their own individual needs, desires, intentions and feelings that are separate from ours — in mind when interacting with them. It is an ability to reflect upon and have a good go at understanding our children's internal experiences (how they might be thinking and feeling, for example), and make connections between their behaviours and feelings. It also requires us to have an awareness of our own internal experience and that our feelings influence our interactions and responses to our kids. So in the tantrum example above, good reflective functioning would be to see the 'tantrum behaviour', stop and think that there is a reason for this behaviour, quickly change positions (mentally) and have a go at understanding how this situation must seem from our young child's point of view. We then respond to them in accordance with the per-

I'M TIRED. I'M HUNGRY. AND THIS SEAT IS VERY HARD!

spective that has been broadened by our efforts to see things from their position.

Arietta Slade talks about how we can approach the relationship with our kids by being curious about their mental states and by having a 'reflective stance', looking for their 'intentions'. This will help us to go beyond responding to their *behaviour* and respond to their *feelings* as well. Perhaps see what happens when you tap into a memory of your child carrying on big time. Tap into your feelings about the behaviour. How do you feel? Annoyed? Embarrassed? Frustrated? Now move beyond the behaviour and understand that your child was carrying on because they were feeling sad and upset that another child hit them and took their favourite toy. Is there a shift in how you feel? Shifting our focus beyond our kids' behaviour in this way, and responding to the 'inside' rather than the 'outside', is what helps us to be sensitive and in tune with them. It's what leads us to interact with them in a way that promotes that sense of security — that sense of being emotionally safe — that might have our little people say to themselves, 'These people really get me.'

And by the way, interacting with them in this way can have great benefits for us as parents as it can foster a deeper sense of closeness. Seeing our children's behaviour as everyone else does, but also making real attempts to see it differently in terms of looking for where it is coming from, leads to that 'the light bulb just switched on' feeling that comes with wider understanding. It's as if we've revealed the real 'truth' about what is going on for them. And it would seem to me that if we kept up trying to understand what is really going on for them, and responded to what we discover instead of just to their 'outside' behaviour, our relationship with our children would blossom as they grow. Who knows what we could learn about our children as people if we kept looking at their behaviour differently? After all, as was famously said by Albert Szent-Györgyi, winner of the 1937 Nobel Prize for Physiology or Medicine, 'Discovery consists of looking at the same thing as everyone else and thinking something different.'

We could discover wonderful vulnerabilities and strengths — qualities that make our children *our* children — if we think to look at them in a certain way.

Approaching our young children, or our children at

My Parenting Values
How I want to be as a parent

— I want to use my 'observing self' as much as possible
— I want to try to see things from their perspective as much as possible

any age for that matter, in this way has to be a conscious choice. It's more of an attitude than a skill. And it will be easier to do if it is part of our parenting values, how we genuinely want to *be* as a parent. Perhaps add it to the list?

Using our observing self to be aware of what our kids see

Just like poor Melody in the cartoon below, we can all get a bit of a surprise when we look in the mirror sometimes. We can discover that the reality of what other people have been looking at is not quite the same as we imagined in our own minds! This is very relevant when it comes to the looks we give our children. I can certainly remember the different expressions my mother used to make when she was showing me her 'emotional repertoire'. But do we really know what our children see? Do we really know what our face looks like when we are showing them our emotional repertoire? Just as we can remember our own parents' looks, our children are downloading *our* looks as we speak, and they will recall them in the future. 'Oh Mum, remember when you were angry?

Oh no! I've got a booger hanging from my nose!

MELODY SUDDENLY REALISES WHY HER DATE DIDN'T COME BACK AFTER SAYING HE HAD TO USE THE RESTROOM.

113

Your eyes went squinty at the edges and your mouth went into a "cat's bum" formation ...' Really?

It would be nice to know what they are viewing and what images they are storing away. We don't see our expressions; we just feel the accompanying emotions. And some of those feelings can make pretty frightening looks appear on our faces. Our children experience the full brunt of our emotional expression. With anger for example, they hear the tone of our voice, the volume of our voice, the words we are saying — all the things we can be aware of as well — but they also get the extra 'kick' of the look on our face. They receive the complete experience, and I think we sometimes forget or don't ever think about that. When we are trying to be mindful of how they are perceiving things to which they are exposed, the looks on our faces and how they see us when we are showing them the potentially scary emotions tend to be overlooked.

So next time you are looking in the mirror, perhaps run through a few expressions. Make them as authentic to your feelings as possible. Get in touch with a time you felt genuinely angry with your kids. Move along the continuum from looking neutral to mildly frustrated to absolutely flabbergasted to the level of anger that's right before you explode and then onto what you look like when you are exploding. Also try this with the more 'positive' emotions: surprised, genuinely excited or laughing so hard you risk peeing your pants. And while doing this, tap into that observing self and really notice what you are seeing in the mirror. Notice the look in your eyes and how your face looks different from the 'normal' non-angry mum/dad/carer. And why not extend it to the whole kit-and-caboodle? Add in the tone and intensity of your voice and say some of the things you would usually say when feeling these feelings. And notice what it physically feels like when you are making those expressions with your face and what your voice sounds like saying those words. Really notice — look and listen.

This is what our kids see and this is what they hear. If we want to be aware of what we look like to *them* and what we sound like to *them* perhaps add it to the 'values' list and use our observing self to check in with what our face looks like from time to time. Making a conscious decision to change expressions might be required if our observing self discovers a less-than-valued expression.

My Parenting Values
How I want to be as a parent

— I want to use my 'observing self' as much as possible
— I want to try to see things from their perspective as much as possible
— I want to be aware of my expressions

Using our observing self to be aware of what we say to our kids

A strong interest of mine lies in how the things we truly believe influence how we think and behave. Sometimes we aren't even aware of these governing forces, but with a little digging they can often be revealed. I have always been intrigued by how these beliefs form and knew it had something to do with the way in which people interacted with us — the things they said to us, the way they treated us — but didn't really know more than that. When I became interested in the perinatal mental health field, I went down a path of learning and on the way I came across a

DVD called *Nature, Nurture and the Power of Love* by cellular biologist Bruce Lipton. On watching this DVD I had a bit of a light-bulb moment about how beliefs are instilled in us.

On his DVD (and also in his book *The Biology of Belief*), Bruce Lipton speaks about how young children are 'programmed' during their first six years of life. He talks about how their biology primes them to be particularly susceptible to download information they are exposed to because of the natural electrical activity level of their brains. To put it simply, brains have brain waves, which are basically brain activity. Brain waves range from slow to active and are called Delta, Theta, Alpha and Beta, with Delta the slowest and Beta the most active. Researchers say that, as children develop, a different brain wave dominates. Between birth and two years of age, the brain predominantly operates at the slowest brain wave (Delta). Between two and six years of age, the brain spends more time at the slightly faster (but still slow) brain wave Theta. After age six children move into beginning to be more conscious in the way they go about things with Alpha as the dominant brain wave, and from age twelve they are using active focused consciousness more, with Beta being the dominant brain wave.

This means that from birth to age six a child's brain is predominantly operating at the slowest brain waves. What is interesting to note is that when the brain is in this state we are more suggestible. In fact, hypnotherapists get people's brain activity to operate at the Delta and Theta level so that they are more programmable. So children are very programmable between birth and the age of six.

So what's being 'programmed'? The simple answer is what they observe, what they see and hear, how they are spoken to and what they are told, how they are interacted with. As a result, as Bruce Lipton points out, their parents' behaviour and beliefs become their own. This is how beliefs are instilled. This was my light-bulb moment.

I've come to understand this as the 'sponge phenomenon', alluding to the saying 'children are like sponges'. It would seem to be the likely process behind the swear-word acquisition technique mentioned in the last chapter, and can offer an explanation for the remarkable ability of children to learn things that they look too little to know. My lovely neighbour told me a story about her son when he was three years old. He asked, 'What does sh-t mean, Mum?' To which she replied, 'It's a not very nice word for poo.' He then corrected her with, 'No it's not. It's a word you use when you can't find something!' Young children are so clever and this story always reminds me that they not only see all and hear all, but they incorporate it all into their understanding of how the world they are growing up in works.

Unfortunately, not all they are exposed to is as lovely and innocent as my neighbour's story. Imagine what is happening to a child if a parent tells her that she is 'stupid' or 'naughty' or that she 'doesn't deserve to have good things' or is 'useless' or 'ugly'. Such comments, if said regularly, are being downloaded into that young child as facts or truths about herself as a person and can unconsciously shape her thinking patterns, behaviours and self-beliefs. And because young children's brains are not developed enough to consider that those comments might have been said 'just out of anger', and that Mum didn't mean it, she hasn't the ability to dispute that they might not be true. It's just the way it is for her. This child's core beliefs CD would play: 'I'm stupid, I'm naughty, I'm not deserving, I'm useless and I'm ugly.'

Conversely, imagine if a child was regularly told she is 'very clever' or 'a good listener' or that she's 'a nice person', 'good at colouring' or 'a caring friend'. *These* are the messages that are being downloaded as facts or truths and can unconsciously shape her self-beliefs and potential through life. She hasn't the brain capability to dispute the accuracy of this information; this is just the way it is for her. Her core beliefs CD would play: 'I'm clever, I'm good at listening, I'm nice, I'm caring and I'm good at colouring.'

These children have received completely different messages and, as a result, are embarking on life with completely different outlooks.

I have done some basic training in hypnosis and one of the things that really stuck with me was the notion of 'waking suggestions'. In hypnosis, suggestions are what the person being hypnotised hears when deeply relaxed in order to bring about a change in something, usually a behaviour or way of thinking. 'You will no longer feel the need to smoke' is an example. Waking suggestions refer to statements that have the same structure as hypnotic suggestions but are not used for the purpose of hypnotising someone. Yet they can have a similar effect and they are said to people all the time as part of normal conversations. They are not intentional, people saying them aren't being nasty; in fact, they are often said out of concern. 'Don't walk on that — you'll fall off!' 'Be careful — you'll cut yourself!' 'You won't be able to do that — you're too quiet.' It's amazing how many of these you hear when you are listening out for them. They're also another thing to think about when speaking to our young kids, especially now that we know they are biologically primed to take in and absorb what is said to them.

Waking suggestions are not all bad, however. On the flip side are those such as: 'Have a go — you can do it!', 'Pay attention to what you're doing and you'll do a good job!', 'You have clever ideas.' It's all in the words we choose and the angle we come from: the negative or the positive.

We can use our observing self to be conscious of what programs are being downloaded into our young children by being aware of what we say to them and the *way* in which we say things to them, how we behave towards them and around them; basically, how we communicate with them. Perhaps add this to the values list too?

That being said, we need to be forgiving of ourselves as well. Occasionally we blow up and say things and behave in ways that we wish we hadn't. The idea is to become *more aware* and this can take some time and learning. Part of the process is to be open to 'repairing' with our children. If something does come out in frustration, we wait until we've calmed down, then send a more positive and accurate message to our children and use the blow-up as part of the learning process towards being more self-observing parents. The concept of repairing is hugely important, basically because it is a matter of either programming the message that came out in anger or programming the modified message that comes with repair. It's so important that it goes on the list.

Using our observing self to be aware of our stress levels

Being stressed makes us particularly vulnerable to having outbursts and blow-ups. I know in our household the stress levels are noticeably lower when we have less on. On the days that are scheduled to the max with multiple places to get to for multiple people, there is more snappiness and incidents of 'speaking loudly'.

When we are stressed there doesn't seem to be time to spare for anything, let alone any of that stress-management malarkey that people like me go on about all the time. But it really doesn't take all that long to lower the stress levels. Really. It benefits all of us to make the effort: our kids for obvious reasons, and us because lowering our stress can put us in a better position to be the things on our 'values' list, the things that matter to us.

Simply being aware of where our stress level is at can have the effect of lowering it. This is where our observing self comes back in. Stepping back and noticing that we are stressed is a necessary thing to do if we want to manage it.

Having a way to think about stress can help us to tap into our observing self. I always use the analogy of a bath when talking about stress to people. And not just any bath but a bath that typifies our individual capacity for stress. So for some it is a small baby bath and for others it is a big deluxe spa bath. Whatever the bath, it has the plug in and when we are stressed the tap is constantly dripping. And what happens when a tap drips into a bath that has the plug in? It fills up. And if the plug isn't taken out, what happens then? It spills over.

So this is how I describe stress. We are the bath with the plug in it. Our various stressors are the dripping tap. If we never take out the plug, there is no other option but for the water to spill over. Stress management is about taking out the plug regularly. This way we keep the level below 'spill over' point.

The way we experience stress depends on many factors, including our personality traits, how we've been taught to deal with stress and our individual life circumstances. While we have little control over these things, we can have some influence over how we manage our stress. We do this by using our observing self to notice we are stressed, that our bath is filling up and that we need to pull out our bath plug.

Noticing we are stressed is one way to pull out the plug because being in the noticing state means we have stepped back from our stress; it takes us from being *in* the stress to *observing* it. The stuff that is causing our stress is still going on — we haven't changed any of that — we are just looking at it from a different position. This is what is called 'defusion' in ACT, going from being 'fused' with the things causing stress to defused from them. It's simply a different way of viewing the same thing.

This is a very useful strategy to have on our stress-management tool belt. Other quick and easy strategies for 'pulling the plug' are deep breathing, self-talk and mindfulness.

Deep breathing requires you to breathe through the nose, slowly and deeply. Perhaps mentally count your breath while breathing in and out: in-two-three-four-five and out-two-three-four-five-six-seven. Try to make the breath as slow and as long and deep as possible. Enlisting visualisation can help with this. Perhaps imagine the breath as a colour that fills your body and gets right down to the bottom of your lungs. Or imagine a deflated balloon in your tummy. As you breathe in, the balloon blows up; as you breathe out, the balloon deflates again. Any visualisation that makes sense to you and helps you focus on taking slow deep breaths is helpful. Deep breathing is very useful as it quickly calms down the body. Adding in visualisation helps because while we are focusing on our breathing, not only are we encouraging a deeper, slower breath, but we also aren't focusing overly on the things causing the stress.

Self-talk is just that: talking to ourselves. What we are trying to do with self-talk is talk ourselves down, give our body a different, non-stressful message to respond to. So instead of continuing with the type of thinking that might escalate the stress, self-talk replaces it with the opposite. We use calm, soothing, simple, reassuring thoughts like, 'It's okay. I'll get through this', 'Take one step at a time', 'Break it down', 'Focus on breathing', 'Keep your eye on the big picture.' Doing this is not unlike soothing a small child — we keep it simple and not 'wordy'; the main aim is to calm and placate. It can be useful to imagine helping a friend to calm down. What sort of things would you say to them?

Mindfulness has a few definitions, but a simple one is 'having full awareness of the present moment'. When we are stressed, our mind is usually full of the stressors and therefore we might not be as aware as we could be of our surroundings or what we are doing. For example, we might be watching TV but our mind might be elsewhere, going over the things causing our stress. We look like we are watching TV but we aren't really. In other words, we are not fully aware of the present moment — we are not 'mindful' of what we are watching on TV or that we are even watching TV. To use mindfulness as a way of 'pulling the plug' (i.e. managing that stress), we fill our mind with something other than the stressors. It can be anything — walking, eating, watching, listening — as long as we are really in the moment, noticing the details of what we are doing. It might also be helpful to nominate and have close at hand something that elicits genuinely calm feelings. But again, using mindfulness means being fully aware that we are looking at a happy holiday snap on a photo board, or a gift our children made at preschool, or an object of some kind that has particular opposite-to-stressed feelings attached to it.

Whatever way we choose to 'pull the plug', it is important to remember that all we're after is a reduction in stress. It's not about taking the stress away — that's a bit unrealistic in the immediate moment. We are still feeling stressed for our various reasons, we

My Parenting Values
How I want to be as a parent

– I want to use my 'observing self' as much as possible
– I want to try to see things from their perspective as much as possible
– I want to be aware of my expressions
– I want to remember they are very programmable and be aware of what I say and do with them
– I want to 'repair' with them
– I want to keep a check on my stress levels

are just trying to flip the balance of power so that it doesn't control and dominate and make us say and do things that we don't really want to or that conflict with our parenting values.

Perhaps add stress-level awareness to the values list?

Something to think about

I remember reading the following in a doctor's surgery long before I became a mother. At the time it made a lot of sense and it struck me just what a responsibility being a parent is. It always stayed with me as a concept that the way children develop has a lot to do with how those around them behave. While I know a little more now and realise there's a bit more to it, I find it still hits the spot. It's a nice reminder to be aware of the messages we send them through our voice, behaviour and actions.

Children Learn What They Live

— Dorothy Law Nolte

If a child lives with criticism, he learns to condemn.

If a child lives with hostility, he learns to fight.

If a child lives with fear, he learns to be apprehensive.

If a child lives with pity, he learns to feel sorry for himself.

If a child lives with ridicule, he learns to be shy.

If a child lives with jealousy, he learns what envy is.

If a child lives with shame, he learns to feel guilty.

If a child lives with encouragement, he learns to be confident.

If a child lives with tolerance, he learns to be patient.

If a child lives with praise, he learns to be appreciative.

If a child lives with acceptance, he learns to love.

If a child lives with approval, he learns to like himself.

If a child lives with recognition, he learns that it is good to have a goal.

If a child lives with sharing, he learns about generosity.

If a child lives with honesty and fairness, he learns what truth and justice are.

If a child lives with security, he learns to have faith in himself and in those about him.

If a child lives with friendliness, he learns that the world is a nice place in which to live.

If you live with serenity, your child will live with peace of mind.

Bibliography

Chugani, H.T., 'Fine-Tuning the Baby Brain', *The Dana Foundation*, <http://www.dana.org/news/cerebrum/detail.aspx?id=1228>, 2004.

Chugani, H.T., Behen, M.E., Muzik, O., Juhasz, C., Nagy, F., and Chugani, D.C., 'Local Brain Functional Activity Following Early Deprivation: A Study of Postinstitutionalised Romanian Orphans', *NeuroImage, 14*, 1290–1301, 2001.

Fogel, A., *Infancy: Infant, Family and Society* (5th Edition), Sloan Publishing, NY 2009.

Gerhardt, S., *Why Love Matters*, Brunner Routledge, East Sussex, 2004.

Harris, R., *ACT Made Simple: An Easy-to-Read Primer on Acceptance and Commitment Therapy*, New Harbinger Publications, Inc., 2009.

Lipton, B.H., *The Biology of Belief: Unleashing the Power of Consciousness, Matter, and Miracles*, Mountain of Love/Elite Books, CA, 2005.

Mares, S., Newman, L., Warren, B., with Cornish, K., *Clinical Skills in Infant Mental Health*, Acer Press, Australia, 2005.

Siegel, D.J., and Hartzell, M., *Parenting from the Inside Out: How a deeper self-understanding can help you raise children who thrive*, Tarcher/Penguin, New York, NY, 2003.

Slade, A., 'Parental Reflective Functioning: An Introduction', *Attachment and Human Development, 7*, 269–281, 2005.

Slade, A., 'Keeping the Baby in Mind: A Critical Factor in Perinatal Mental Health', <www.zerotothree.org>, 2000.

Winnicott, D.W., *The Child, the Family and the Outside World*, Penguin Books, Harmondsworth, Middlesex, 1978 (original work published 1964).

Zeanah, C.H. (ed.), *Handbook of Infant Mental Health* (3rd Edition), The Guilford Press, NY, 2009.

Acknowledgements

I have the deepest gratitude for the team at Exisle Publishing, especially Gareth, Benny and Anouska, for giving me the opportunity to publish this book on a topic I am very passionate about — thank you.

A big thank you to Simon Goodway for the absolutely fabulous cartoons scattered throughout the pages.

I'd like to acknowledge all the professionals and authors whose talks I have attended and whose books I've read for the part they've played in developing my passion for the topics in this book.

And to my family and supporters — thank you for giving me the time to write.

Index